HOW TO INTERPRET YOUR DREAMS FROM A - Z

By HENRY BOULANGER

A Citadel Press Book
Published by Carol Publishing Group

First Carol Publishing Group Edition 1990

A Citadel Press Book
Published by Carol Publishing Group
Citadel Press is a registered trademark of Carol Communications, Inc.

Editorial Offices: 600 Madison Avenue, New York, NY 10022
Sales & Distribution Offices: 120 Enterprise Avenue, Secaucus, NJ 07094
In Canada: Canadian Manda Group, P.O. Box 920, Station U, Toronto,
Ontario, M8Z 5P9, Canada

Queries regarding rights and permissions should be addressed to:
Carol Publishing Group, 600 Madison Avenue, New York, NY 10022

Manufactured in the United States of America
ISBN 0-8065-0991-0

Carol Publishing Group books are available at special discounts
for bulk purchases, for sales promotions, fund raising, or
educational purposes. Special editions can also be created to
specifications. For details contact: Special Sales Department,
Carol Publishing Group, 120 Enterprise Ave., Secaucus, NJ 07094

15   14   13   12   11   10   9   8   7   6   5   4

PREFACE

Explanation of the dream version is as old as the dream itself. To think about every unusual occurrence is inherent to human nature, and so it was with the first dream man had. After they had experienced a picture that they had seen in a dream, their vision was very often fulfilled in real life. In this respect it was an omen for them. You can read by Homer (a Greek poet of 600 B.C.), about the old heroic line who used to fight about the town of Troja and the dream pictures they had. They thought these visions were an inspiration from God, so all of their actions were built up in connection with the visions of their dreams. In the old testament of the Holy Bible we can find a very complete interpretation of dreams. We can read of some unusual dreams which became the truth word for word. Furthermore, we can learn from some of the famous dream interpreters, such as Joseph and Daniel. We also know that in the palaces of Egypt, Persia and Babylon an appointed class of people systematically studied the dreams of man and interpreted them.

Dreams begin through the activity of our soul. To clarify this, I will give a short explanation: any perception which leads to our senses will be received through our nerves, which in turn send messages to our soul. The nerves (which are like very fine threads), are distributed to all parts of the body and are connected with the eyes, ears, tongue, nose, fingers and toes. Finally, the nerves converge in the brain. As long as the nerves are in a state of tension, we are in a state of awakefulness. The slightest impression of a certain stimulus can influence the body. With an unbelievable speed, this impression will be passed on to the brain and immediately the image of this sensation arises. For example: as soon as a sound enters the ear, the ear nerve vibrates, similar to a tight guitar string. The sound travels with an incredible speed to our brain, where the nodal point for all of our nerves is located. In our brain we perceive the sound. The ear is the external tool for catching sounds and words like an amplifier on the nerves. This same situation we experience with the eyes, tongue, nose and all of the other parts of the body. The only purpose of these superficial resources is to transmit impressions to our soul.

But those external auxiliaries, (ear, eye and so on) are not absolutely necessary to catch impressions. The soul receives the power of sensation through our nerves, and perceptions also originate through our thoughts. The result is power of the faculty of imagination, and this is our fantasy. How often we have fantasized of a happy future of pleasant endings to problems and never seen those pictures with our own eyes, but we see them clear and picture-like as if they are real. We may ask ourselves: what is it? We did not see it with our eyes, nevertheless, it is very real to us. Therefore, why should it not be possible for the soul to feel perceptions while our body is in a sleeping state.

Already, we have learned that the eye is not absolutely necessary to receive pictures. This is a fact. In the same manner, the fantasies we have while in an awake state lead to fantasies while in a sleeping state, which we call dreams. Fantasies during the awake state are very similar to the fantasy of a dream. Therefore, is it possible that a person deeply involved with his thoughts is dreaming with his eyes open? Yes, he is. The only difference with a dream in a state of awakefulness (a daydream), is that you are able to interrupt the succession of fantasy pictures, put them in order, change, or completely destroy them.

The process of dreaming while in a sleeping state is a completely different situation, because we are not able to interrupt or change any of our dreams, as we have no control of our impulses. While sleeping the soul has an uninterrupted series of conceptions and fantasies. Sometimes we cannot remember our dreams; they were weak and mixed up, and by the time we awaken, we do not have the slightest idea what they were all about. It has been said that in the case of great fatigue, we do not dream at all. This is not true, and it is wrong to say that there is no sensitivity or that there is complete inactivity of the soul. The power of perception of a dream by great emission of our nerve cells may frequently weaken, therefore we may not remember a dream. The soul by itself is never indolent. From the moment it was created and united with the human body, the performance of the soul was always actual. The human body needs rest and sleep. Not so for the soul; a change in activity is its refreshment. New circumstances and events increase the activity of our soul. As long as a human being is awake, his mind is a powerful ruler over his soul. With our willpower we have the capability to break the activity of our soul, and it has no chance to be independent. To a great extent while you are asleep, the activity of the mind is in a state of unconsciousness. In other words, the mind has been subdued. Now the soul has complete freedom to function.

In a dream the soul's activity is more widespread and free. On the contrary, in a conscious condition, faculty of judgment and the view of position on all the matters and conclusions for the future are clear and not constrained as they would otherwise appear under the restraints of the delusive senses and the instability of the will. I believe that everybody has had this experience at one time or another.

A problem occurred during the day and seemed insoluble before bedtime. During the night while sleeping, all that you experienced that day fits more clearly into perspective the following morning. Then you ask yourself: how could I get so disturbed yesterday? In simple terms, the soul while resting continues its thoughts and follows the problem more clearly, which was denied during the awake condition. Out of all this, the soul's prominent activity during sleep was to continue the solving of the problem that occurred prior to retiring for the night.

We know from earlier explanations that the language of dreams during sleep is completely different from the language of the awakened condition. While the soul is in a dream; in a much higher liberal sphere, the language is more idealistic and symbolic. To find a key to understanding the meaning of this language is the purpose of the interpretation of dreams. The difference of significant or unimportant dreams was already recognized in earlier times, but the cause of dreams was not described until much later on. We are positive that in dreams where figures and characteristics frequently change and where everything is in chaos, that there is no kind of connection or meaning. When we lie restless, tossing and turning, in our dreams being chased, or falling from one danger into another, our dreams are most likely responsible and they are influenced by our health and mental condition. The consumption of heavy meals or large quantities of alcohol may also contribute to restless sleep and confusing dreams. Another version of dreams may occur after you have read exciting literature or had a stimulating conversation. We may relive the moments in our dreams again as a confusing and exaggerated variation of a view, as it actually took place earlier. I call those dreams meaningless. They do not contribute to any more specific interpretation.

Nevertheless, we are able to make a successful explanation of a dream which is remembered and has had no extraordinary suppositions.

Melanchthon (theology reformer and teacher from 1497-1560) was one of the first men who had the ingenuity and courage to talk and to write about the explanation of dreams and to appear publicly. Another person who ventured to probe the meanings of dreams was Heironimus Cordamus. In 1562 his essay about dreams was published and widely read in Europe. The modern theories, knowledge and research in the field of psychology that initially connected psychoanalysis with personal psychology is worthy of great praise and recognition. We now understand that experiences from the past may recur in our dreams. A present event will vanish into a state of subconsciousness, but it may have a presentiment of the future.

This book should be of help. This modern version has been derived from the basics of Assyrian and Babylonian interpretations. It is entirely up to the individual to decide whether the data from this literature has any value for his or her own translation into the psychology of dreams. Everyone's day dream is to be and stay healthy, to have success in business, employment, in love and marriage, and to be safe from the dangers which surround us day and night and, finally, to give us the power of good judgment and the ability of leadership. Each and everyone's goal must be to trust your own conscience and to find fulfillment in your own life. This book is meant to be a guideline for you.

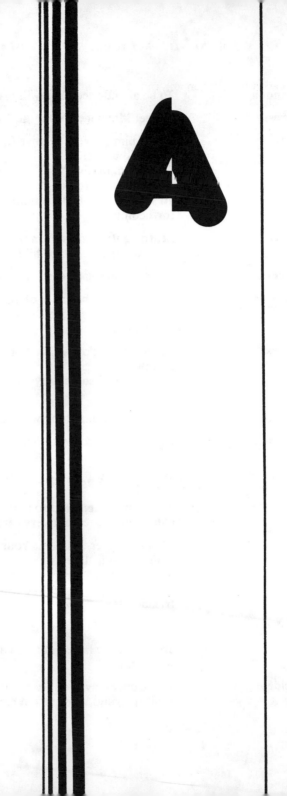

Abandon	To be abandoned: You will reach your goal.
Abbess	To see: Marriage within the family.
Abbot	To see him pray: A relative far away is ill and soon will be well again. To see him in his gown: Watch out for an underhanded crook. To see him give benediction: To find good forthcoming.
A B C	Learning it: Undergo a new acquisition. Reading it: Teachable children.
Abject	To be: Unpleasant surprises to come.
Abortion	To have one: The cause of your agitation is not as serious as it seems to be. Your opinion will change.
Abscess	To have one: You will be bothered by unpleasant persons. To see one on somebody: A standstill in your business life.
Absinthe	To drink it: Something will worry you.
Abstinence	Resist an urge to try to balance your budget by gambling.
Abyss	To see one: A warning of a threatening accident. To fall into one: Lead to a hazardous health condition - watch out very carefully.
Acacia	Walking under the trees: Your most desired wish will come true. Seeing the blossoms and picking them: You will be disappointed in the trust of your friends.
Academy	To be in one: Your outlook on people is grim.
Accessories	To see a set or have one: You are in for a big surprise.
Accident	To see one: Have confidence in yourself. While playing: Unexpected recognition.

Accordion	To see or hear one: Reconciliation is in the near future.
Accounts	To see one: You will reach a pleasant goal. To keep one: You receive an offer of a good job.
Accuse	Means: Keep your mouth closed.
Accused	To become: Health problems should not affect your performance at work in any way today. To be: You will be pleased to discover that your associates are cooperative.
Accuser	To be one: Haughtiness and discontentment. To see one: Money expenses.
Achilles tendon	To see one: You will get into deep trouble if you don't change your lifestyle.
Acid	To work with: Be aware of a problem which may be forthcoming. To be hurt by it: Mild sickness.
Acorns	To see them: A good friend will lend you a helping hand.
Actor	To see one: You will have to spend money.
Adam and Eve	To see them: Thoughts of romance may interfere with your ability to concentrate on your work today.
Adder	To see one: This is a warning to be aware of danger.
Addition	To do it: You will receive news.
Adjutant	To become one: There is a new project in sight.
Admiral	To see or speak to one: You can expect an important message from overseas.
Admire	If you do: Sadness and worries within your family life.
Adopt	If you adopt: You will take over responsibilities.

	If someone adopts you: You will gain favoritism from your boss.
Adore	If you worship someone: You will do things on impulse.
Adorn	If a joyous person sees another or himself adorned: Be seriously warned if you want to protect your goods and health.
Adultery	To do: Something is wrong in your surroundings. People are trying to betray you, but you are not yet aware of it.
Adventure	Coming through it unharmed: You are prone to danger.
Advertisement	To read one: There is news coming your way. To make one: Your hopes will not be realized.
Advice	To give it: Boring lawsuits. To receive it: Repay with ingratitude. To hear it: Instinctively you will do the right thing.
Advocate	To see one: You will receive a letter from the court. If you are in close contact with a friend of one: A dispute will occur with friends or family members. This dream warns you to be cautious.
Affliction	To suffer one: A small loss.
Afraid	To be: You may be insulted.
Africa	To be in or on a safari: You may go on a journey or have a change of address.
Afterpiece	To see or to work with one: Pleasant advancement in the future. To lose one: You are scared.
Agate	Its appearance in a dream means: Luck in your love affair.
Age	To be of old age: Honor and dignity. To dream of old people: You will receive ad-

vice from an older person.
To dream of a gray-haired man: Good luck.
To see an old building: You will have contempt shown you.

Agent
To negotiate with one: You will influence someone.
To see one: You may lose some property.
To become one: You may overcome barriers.

Agriculture
To see it: If you must sign legal documents, seek expert advice about any terms you don't fully understand.

Agricultural Tools
Seeing or handling the tools: You may take over a business.

Ague
To have it: Improve your health by changing your eating habits.

Airplane
To see one: Good news concerning money will be received from an unusual source.

Airport
To see one: An important move should be postponed.

Alabaster
To touch it: You cherish false hopes.

Alarm
To hear one: You will receive good news.
To hear a trumpet: Do not hesitate with your plans.
To hear a beat: Good luck in business.

Album
To look in one: Your life will change.

Alcove
To be in one: Commotion and discontentment.

Alibi
To present an alibi: Officials will contact you.

Alimony
To receive: You are well off.
To pay: Unfavorable occurrence.

Alive
To be buried: An unlucky omen.
To be burned: Is a sign of uneasiness and of war.

Alley
To be in or see one: Happiness.
To sweep one: Sadness or trouble.

Alligator	To see one: You should discuss your problems with close relatives.
Allowance	Dreaming about one: You will be hindered in your undertakings.
Almanac	To read one: You will make connections with the financial community.
Almonds	To eat them: Don't worry; everything will be all right.
Almond tree	In blossom: Your wishes will come true.
Alms	To give to the poor: Good luck. To give to the sick: Trouble and uncertainty. To receive: This is normally a sign of dishonor and distress.
Aloe	Long life with good health.
Alpine dairy maid	You will receive an invitation to a festival.
Altar	To see one: Hopes and luck. To kneel in front of one: Your dream will be fulfilled.
Alteration	Of clothing: There will be a great turnaround in your life.
Alum	Misfortune in your undertakings.
Aluminum	To see it: Someone will make you a reasonable offer.
Amazon	To see one: An unhappy marriage.
Amber	To see a stone: You will receive a gift. To own amber jewellery: You will meet conceited women.
Ambitious	To be: Be alert - somebody will test you.
Ambulance	To see one: People are ungrateful to you.
America	To travel in: You will escape unpleasantness.
Ammonia	To smell it: Bad news from a faraway place.
Amulet	To find one: Approaching marriage. To wear one: Break up of hostile attacks.

Amusement	To witness it: Curb your loose tongue.
Anaesthesia	Something will cause annoyance.
Ancestor	To see them: You will damage a relative's relationship.
Anchor	To see one: A friendship will strengthen. To throw one: Great danger. A broken one: A loss of a dear friend or lover.
Anchovy	To eat one: Someone wants something for nothing.
Anecdote	To relate to one: Your companionship is questionable.
Angels	To see: The future will tell your friends that you are not as bad as they thought you were. To hear them sing: Your yearning will be fulfilled. To talk to them: Your position would be better if you would follow a straight path. To be one yourself: Many of your friends do not believe in you because of your arrogance. To hear them talk: An ill acquaintance will die. To see them dance: You will receive unexpected good news. To see them playing instruments: Honor and dignity.
Anger	To have it: A lot of happiness is in sight. To be angry in your dream: Some unpleasant situation will occur. Be prepared and handle it calmly.
Animals	To tame: Jealousy. To hear them talk: Don't be quite so frank. Wild ones: Unexpected good luck.
Anniversary	To celebrate one: The coming years will be the most successful of your life.
Annoyance	With neighbors: Avoid hypocrites and flatterers - they are only interested in your downfall.

With a superior: Your diligence will be rewarded.

With your wife: An important domestic adjustment may occur which could include beautification of your surroundings.

With your husband: You will dig beneath the surface and the dilemma will be solved.

With next of kin: You will make the correct choice, and a family reunion is in sight.

With a brother: Your stubborn associate has your best interests at heart.

With a sister: If you are patient, what you need will be handed to you on the proverbial silver platter.

With a clergyman: It will make your life more pleasant if you obey the ten commandments.

With old women: Through your own fault you get into quarrels.

With a stranger: Don't try to gain money if the acquisition involves any danger.

Annual fair   It is better to save some money, than to save none at all.

Answer   To give one: Wisdom.

Antichrist   To see an atheist: You will undergo a bad alliance.

Ant   To see one: You will do more work for less pay.

Antelope   To see one: Gain through speculation.

Ant hill   To step into one: You will get involved with the wrong crowd.

Antlers   To buy them: There are untruths between you and your spouse.
To see them: Be cautious.

Anvil   To use one: You will become wealthy.
To see one: Your friends will disappoint you.

Apartment   To have one: Your diligence will lead you to your goal.
A poor one: Your situation will get better.

To rent one: Don't lose your courage.

Apostate   Means highest despair and disorder of the mind.
You are close to corruption.

Apostle   You will become a godparent.

Appeal   You will build up false hopes.

Appetite   To have one: Scarcity of money.

Applause: To give it: You won't hold a grudge.
To receive it: You will become vain.

Apple   To eat a sour one: You will agree on an unpleasant situation.
To eat a sweet one: There is a joyful message forthcoming.

Apple blossom   To see one: Good news and a happy love life.

Apple cider   To drink it: You may undergo medical treatment.

Apple tree   To see one: Joy and amusement are forthcoming.

Appliance   To see one: You will have good luck in all of your ventures.

Apprentice   To be one: Your success will be rapid.

Apricots   To see them: Winning and happiness are forthcoming.
To eat them: You will have a good marriage.

Apron   To see one: A very interesting person will visit you.

Aquarium   You will experience inconvenience.

Aqueduct   To see one: In the future you will be an important public figure.

Arab   To see one: An unresolved problem will be cleared up.

Arch-like Building   To see one or to stand in one: You have a faithful spouse.

Archbishop	To see or be with this noble person: Always reveal important news promptly.
Architect	To be with one: Be aware in your business affairs.
Aries	To see: You should think the matter over.
Aristocratic title	To receive one: Bitter deception. If you deal with aristocrats: You will achieve honor. To be an aristocrat: Through your domination of others you will experience loss.
Ark	To see one: You will be irritated.
Armband	This is a very uncommon dream, but if it does appear: Sickness lies ahead.
Armchair	To see one: Sickness.
Arms	To have an injured arm or elbow: Sadness. To have large arms: Hard labor. To have small arms: Becoming poor. To break one: An accident may happen. To have hairy arms: A lot of wealth. To see thin arms: Death.
Armor	To see it: You will be surprised at what knowledge can do for you. If you wear it (man): You may become a soldier. If you wear it (woman): You are running the household.
Armored car	To see one: You will be embarrassed.
Armorer	To see one: Get together with someone who shares your basic interests.
Army	To see one: Agitation and fear. Foreign: Unusual things will happen in your country. To see a marching: Good income.
Arrack	To drink: You are protecting false hopes.
Arrested	To be: Your suspicions are groundless.
Arrival	There will soon be a pleasant surprise.

Arrow	To have one: You will live a lonely life. To throw: You will lose a loved one.
Art gallery	To visit one: Put your faults aside.
Artillery	To see one or to be an artilleryman: Troublesome work.
Ascend	You will definitely reach your goal.
Ashes	To see them: There will be a bitter experience in the future. To spread them: Mourning over a loved one's death.
Ashlar	To see: Hard times in front of you.
Asparagus	To eat it: Your future will be quiet and happy.
Assassinated	To be: Your sorrows will soon be over.
Aster	To see: Nobility and honor.
Astronomy	Dreaming of stars: You will further your education.
Attic	To see one: A relationship will reach a serious level.
Attic window	To see one: Be aware enough to protect your interests. To look through a garret window: Your hopes are farfetched.
Attire	Means: You will discover a hidden secret.
Attorney	To see one: A friend will ask you for advice.
Auction	To hold one: Sickness or death.
Auctioneer	To see one: You will become associated with pleasant company.
Audience	With a noble person: Always reveal important news promptly.
Aunt	There is an inheritance in sight.
Auricula	A full one: Luck in a lottery.
Aurochs	To see: Any obstacles to the path of true love will be removed.

Avalanche

To see one: You will become annoyed with your partner or co-workers.

Avenue

To walk down one: You will receive an unexpected inheritance.
To see one: You will live a long life.

Aversion

Do not take your dreams lightly - be very cautious.
This dream warns you of a disastrous situation ahead.

Awake

Dreaming of waking up: Satisfaction.
To awaken someone: You are worried about a loved one's future.
If you awaken from a noisy dream and are scared, you may have some trouble with your work or health.

Awakening

Don't think about changing your job. You may get yourself into trouble.

Awl

To see: In case of sickness it is better to see your physician.

Axe

To see one that is sharp and shiny: A threatening danger lies ahead.
To have one in your hand: An accident will occur through your negligence.
It also means: Quarrels with close friends or relatives.

Axel

From a wagon: A good project lays ahead of you.

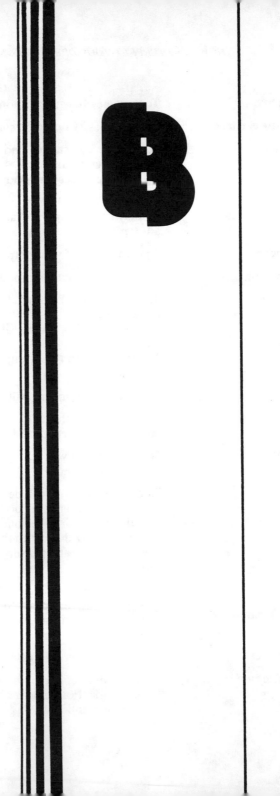

Baby   To see a newborn: Your home is your castle.

Baby carriage   To see one: Try not to be careless today.

Bachelor   To be one: You cannot find fulfillment in your present occupation.
To see one: There are good times ahead for you.

Backgammon   To play it: Pass up the chance to commit adultery.

Bacon   To eat it: One of your patrons will fade away.

Bacteria   To see it: Imaginary sickness.

Badger   To capture one: You will change your homestead.
To see one: It is a symbol of finding a true friend.
To feed one: Don't pay any attention to gossip.

Baggy trousers   To see them: Someone will make fun of you.

Bagpipes   To play or hear them: There will be some countryside entertainment.

Bailiff   To see one: You will have good luck in all of your dealings.

Bake   To bake bread: You will be freed from troubling times and there are good times ahead.
To bake a cake or to see one being made: A family affair will occur in the near future, one in which the dreamer is very closely involved with.

Bakery   To see a bakery or a baker: A blessed year.
To see a kneading trough full of dough: An unexpected inheritance will befall the dreamer.

Balance   Dangerous undertakings.

Balcony   To stand on one: A reunion for lovers.
To see yourself or another about to fall from one: Danger and loss.

Bald head	To see one: Speculation is especially hazardous. Therefore, spending must be moderate. You picture yourself as bald: Treachery will cost you much time and trouble. Be cautious.
Ball	To play: Trouble between you and your acquaintances. To see one: You will reconcile with an enemy. To see others play: Pleasant news is forthcoming. To present or receive one: Unexpected happiness is in sight.
Ball (dance)	To attend one: Engagement or wedding. To see one: You will find amusement. To dance at one which is bright and well decorated: You have a sensational career ahead of you.
Ballerina	Unnecessary expenses.
Ballet	To see one: Enormous deception and disturbance.
Balloon	To see one: Show your energy. To take off in one: You are capable of mastering your own destiny. To see children playing with them: You are capable of making new inventions.
Ballot box	To see one: As long as you remain unapproachable, family differences remain irreconcilable. To see one buried: You will lead a long life.
Balsam fragrance	To smell it: Recovery for the sick, if sick; and if well, you will have a business interruption.
Banana	A ripe one: Pleasant surprise. An overripe one: Unpleasantness ahead.
Bandage	To be bandaged: You will lose your freedom. To see somebody with one: You will continue a lawsuit.
Bandit	Someone will tell lies behind your back.

Bang	To hear one: You will be terrified by unwelcome news.
Banjo	To play one: A particular matter must be finished.
Bank	To have business at one: Be aware of loss through swindlers or erratic speculation. To work at a bank: You will win money. To see a banker: Beware of speculation. To see paper currency: A loss is just ahead of you.
Bankruptcy	The annoyance you feel for your co-workers will grow stronger.
Banner	To carry one: You have a secret admirer. To see one: You will be blessed with happiness.
Banquet	To have one in your house: A family affair will take place which includes some dignitaries. To go to one: You will be unexpectedly honored. You sit at the table: Don't be extravagant. To see one: You will become rich and powerful.
Baptism	To see one: An influential person is willing to give you some excellent advice. To attend one: Excellent company.
Bar	Being in a tavern: Money loss.
Barber	To see one: You are being ignored by the world. To get a haircut or a shave: You will suffer damage.
Barefoot	Walking: Loss of weight and impending poverty.
Bark	To hear a dog bark (without seeing him): Be aware of an unknown danger. To see him bark: Ignore gossip and listen to warning voices.
Bark (tree)	Your wealth will grow because you are ambitious.

Barley   To see it: You will accumulate a fortune.

Barmaid   To see one: Don't destroy your luck.

Barn   To see a full one: Signifies a large inheritance
                      or a good marriage.
                      To see an empty one: You will suffer a disad-
                      vantage.

Barometer   To look at one: One of your friends will never
                      show his true face.

Barracks   To see them: Somebody will try to borrow
                      money from you.
                      To be in one: You will see the world.

Barrel   To broach one: Your suffering will soon be
                      over.
                      To see a leaky one: Warns of a business loss.
                      To see an empty one: Beware of fraud.

Barrel Organ   Do everything possible to keep peace at home.

Baseball   To play: An unpleasant incident.
                      To watch a game of: A joyful and happy time.
                      To see children playing: A happy homelife.

Baseball Bat   To swing one: You will silence envious people.
                      To throw or drop one: Don't start anything
                      you can't finish.

Bashful   To be: Be on the alert for tempting situations.

Basin   Made of porcelain: The loss of a person you
                      hold dear brings you grief.
                      Made of brass or copper: Truth is showing.
                      To wash yourself in a basin: You will admit
                      your mistakes.
                      A silver or gold one: Good luck.

Basket   To see one: Your worries may increase.
                      To plait one: Creative work may cause
                      unusual expense.
                      To empty one: There is a bright future in store
                      for you.

Basketball   To play: An unforeseen inheritance.

Bass singer   To sing: Lust for hearty drinks.

To play a bass: You will reveal yourself as a laughing stock.
To see one play: You make your own happiness.

Bastard   You have loose or wanton ideas.

Bat   To see it: Possess your soul in patience; you will make it.

Bath   In the tub: Acute sickness occurs.
In a brook: Getting over a sickness.
In a river: Strength and perseverance.
In an open pool: You may find a wealthy fiancé or fiancée.
In a room: Untruthfulness.
To take one with soap: Pleasant occurrence.
In deep water: Be careful.
To see a bath: Distress.
To be in lukewarm water: Prosperity.
To be in warm water: Watch out for a cold or chill.
With clothes on: Not feeling well.
In contaminated water: You will bring harm to yourself.

Bathroom   To be in one: You will receive sad news.

Bathsponge   To wash yourself with one: This means that the dreamer has a total sense of well-being.

Bathtub   To see one: This is a symbol of freeing yourself from possible grief and trouble by using your ambition.

Battering ram   Don't worry; everything will work out.

Battle   To fight one: Make peace with your enemies.

Battle ship   To see one: Your intellectual curiosity is highly developed.

Bay leaf   To see one: A chance occurrence will change your life.

Bayonet   To find one: You may become a soldier.
To lose one: Disgrace.

Bay tree   To see one: You can't buy happiness. The

most valuable things in life are free.

Bazaar   You make some unnecessary expenditures.

Beacon light   To see one: You should be cautious in your business affairs.

Beach   To see one: Soon you will travel.

Beads   To have or see them: There will be danger in your life.
To buy them: Loss or sadness.
To play with them: Mild sickness may require the help of a doctor.

Beadle   To have a full one: You will enjoy a good income.

Beam (light)   To see one: Expand your horizons, but do not spread yourself too thinly.

Beam   To sit on one: A secure means of livelihood.

Beans   To see beanstalks growing: You can look forward to a satisfying future.
To cut, cook or eat green beans: Trouble between married couples or lovers.
To eat white beans: Much trouble with family and neighbors.
To plant beans: Good luck in business affairs.

Bear   To see one in the wilderness: Be aware of unscrupulous people who are trying to do you harm.
To see a dead bear or a bearskin: Happiness in the future.
To see more than one: Bad business.

Beard   To have your beard shaved: Insecurity.
Seeing a white beard: Honorable future.
Seeing a red beard: This is an omen of quarrels, fights and false friends.
To shave someone else's beard: You harmed someone unintentionally.
If a beard is unusually long: Your wealth will increase.
If a girl dreams she has a beard: She is losing her lover.

If a beard is burning: Your desired impression will be accomplished.
A thin beard: Mockery.
A pointed beard: You have a loose tongue.
To be beardless: Bad accomplishments ahead.
To see a woman with a beard: You will be involved in an argument.

Beat

To beat someone: An emotional dilemma is resolved.
To receive a beating: You make a valuable contact.
To see a child being beaten: You will suffer from negligence and ignorance.

Beautiful lady

Don't get involved in forbidden matters.

Beaver

To see one: Through passion and hard work the future will be good.
To see a beaver-dam: You are able to hold onto your belongings.

Bed

To make a bed: You will begin a new business.
To see or buy a bed: Be careful in making new deals or in undertaking new tasks.
To see an empty one: Hard times lie ahead.
To see a clean and pretty bed: True love from your partner.
To see a dirty, unmade bed: Untruthfulness and shame.

Bed bug

To have them: A big conflict with someone.

Bedroom

To see one: Pleasant family life.

Bed spread

To put one on a bed: The thing you desire is beyond the scope of your earnings.

Beef

To buy it: Good business connections in the near future.
To cook it: Something will disappoint you.
To eat it: You will be rewarded.

Beer

To pour it into a glass: You will enjoy a good income.
To see a light beer: You will receive a confidential letter.

	To see or drink a flat beer: Sickness and trouble.

Beer stein   To see it full: Happiness.

Bees   To see a beehive: Happiness and honor are forthcoming.
To see a queen bee: Quarrels and jealousies between sweethearts.
To see a swarm of: You may travel far in order to settle an unpleasant affair.
To be stung by a bee: Be aware of false gossip.

Beetles   To see them: Your modesty makes you many good friends.
To catch them: Don't let your success go to your head.

Beets   To eat them: You must overcome some difficulties in order for your dilemma to be resolved.

Begging   To see yourself: You will lose your assets.
To turn a beggar away: Be aware of misfortune and trouble.
To give a handout to a beggar: Reward for a good deed.
To see a beggar entering a house: Uncomfortable situation.
To scold a beggar: You will receive a present.
To pat a beggar: Troubled future.

Bells   To see one: Your endeavor is risky.
To hear them chime: A favorable omen for a current business dealing.
To see them being made: Soon you will begin your own family.
To hear sleigh-bells: Being helpful and considerate to others will do much to improve your image.

Bellows   To see one: Be careful of thoughtless friends who are likely to use your honesty to your disadvantage.
To touch one: Trouble.
To see one in motion: This warns you to vent your anger.

Putting it in motion yourself: Rage surrounds you.

Belt A golden one: Wealth.
To find one: You earn someone's trust.
To lose one: Your love life is going sour.

Bench To see or sit on one: Tiring work leads to inner peace and calmness.

Benediction To give it to someone: Although it doesn't look good now, the situation will improve.

Benefit Render to a person: An occasional splurge will not ruin your budget.

Beneficiary To see one: Quarrel at home.

Berries To pick them: Troublesome work.

Berth To see or be in it: Avoid being misled by false flatterers.

Besiege To dream about war and siege: Most likely you were upset and went to bed worrying about something.
Excess food and drink may also cause violent dreams such as this one.

Bet To win one: If you admit your faults and shortcomings, people will help you.
To lose one: Do not underestimate the power of your own personality.

Betray To be betrayed: Your troubles will multiply.

Bewitched To be: Don't pay so much attention to strangers.

Bible To see or read it: Your home atmosphere is happy.

Bicycle To see one: Count on family members playing an important role in the decisions you make.
To ride one: Surprising good news.
To see an overturned one: Discontent is within yourself.

Bier To see: Family differences will be settled.

Bilberries	To eat them: You will be betrayed in love.
Billiard	To see one: Sick people get well and lovers get married. To play: You are tending to be frivolous. To see a billiard ball: Your happiness is changeable.
Billy-goat	To be kicked by one: You will argue with a rival. To see one jump: You will play some big tricks. To see one: Through human nature, you will cause an undesirable situation.
Birch tree	To climb one: You will experience happiness. To see some trees: You will be punished for something you did in the past.
Birds	To see them fly: Take measures to improve your health. To see them in a cage: A burnt child dreads the fire. To feed them: A sick friend will ask you for help - do not deny him.
Bird's egg	To see: You should think of setting aside more time for rest and relaxation.
Bird's foot	To see one: Your health will improve if you exercise.
Bird's nest	To see: Delayed affairs may be successfully concluded.
Bird of prey	To catch one: For rich people, anger; for poor people, luck.
Birth	To give birth to a child: If you follow a straight path, all of your hopes will be fulfilled. To be present at one: Devote more time to planning your future.
Birthday	To celebrate one: Bright and happy days are ahead.

Birthmark	Bad news about your child.
Biscuit	You have a sweet tooth.
Bishop	To see one: Warning of quarrels and unhappiness. To see a mitre: You will make a testament. To see a crosier: Reconcile with an enemy.
Bite	From a dog: You will lose a court action, and will feel prejudiced. From a person: Continuous protection. From a snake: You are surrounded by deceitful people. From a cat: A lot of hostility with friends and relatives. From a horse: Be aware of a particular person with a deceitful mind.
Biting	Biting out a tooth: You may receive sad news.
Bitter items	To enjoy bitter sweets: Means good health.
Bivouac	You will overcome all of your struggles.
Blackberries	To pick or eat them: Fulfill your plans first, and then enjoy.
Blackbird	To see or hear one sing: You will take a position of honor and status.
Blackboard	To write on one: Don't borrow any money - it will be very difficult to pay it back.
Black market	To witness, buy or sell: As a merchant, business will deteriorate. An employer: You may face unemployment.
Blacksmith	Success and luck.
Blackthorn	To see: Happiness and excitement.
Blanket	To see a pretty quilt or blanket: You may receive a gift from a loving person. To spread out a blanket: Take a chance.
Bleached cloth	You will be exonerated from a false accusation. For young girls: You will likely marry soon.
Bleed to death	Family member aids in special promotion.
Blend	Something: Be on the alert for a swindle.
Blessing	To receive one: You will live to a very old age.

To give one: Follow your instincts; your ability to remain calm under trying conditions will be tested. Control your temper.

Blind   To become blind: Beware of danger.
To guide a blind person: An impending adventurous journey.
To see blind people: You are being delayed in your undertakings.

Blood   To see bloodshed: Haste costs you unpleasantness.
To see it flow: Means sickness.
To see blood from an animal saved: Big business is on its way.
To see someone's face bloody: This person is in great danger.
To see your own hands bloody: Your profits are derived from wrongdoings.

Blood-leech To see one on yourself: If sick, you will soon be well. If well, watch out for illness.
To see one on another person: Watch out for deceitful people; they want to interfere with and take over your life.

Blood-pudding To eat it: You are harming someone.
To cut it: You are exposed to ridicule.

Blood-transfusion To see one: An extraordinary honor will befall you.

Blow-pipe   To use one: Be careful - this is a warning of an accident.

Blush   A career boost is on the agenda.

Boar   To see one: Attention: Someone has the intention of suing you.
To hunt one: You attend to a group of people whom you have misgivings about.

Boat   To be in one: This is telling us that a water voyage is in the future.
To see many: A friend or family member is coming across the water to visit you.

Boating   To see someone: A pleasant surprise is in store.

Boil   To see: Romance will bring you happiness.

Boiler   To see one: Misunderstandings between family members.

Bolt	A door: There is a long and unpleasant journey ahead.
Bomb	To explode one: There is disappointment in your undertaking.
Bond	To see one: Unexpected money.
Bone	To nibble on one: You may find that you are left to your own devices. To see them: You will solve a mystery.
Bonnet	To see one: A wedding. To wear one: Motherhood.
Books	To read one: Knowledge and happiness. To write one: Good fortune and an honorable position. To buy one: You and others will profit. To sell a book: Your outcome will not be as profitable as you originally expected. To write in a book: Your mind is troubled and you are worried about something.
Bookstore	To be in one: Gossip will defame you.
Booth	Being at a fairground surrounded by them: This is an unsettling and troubled time in business. For a farmer: Good trade. For young girls: Pleasant and happy future.
Boots	To put them on: You will be humiliated.
Born	To dream of being born: For rich folks, bad times; For poor folks, better times.
Borrow	Something: Your independence is in jeopardy. To lend money to a friend: You may lose money (and a friend).
Bottle	To see one: Annoyance with your neighbor. To break into pieces: Grief will threaten you.
Bound	To feel yourself bound down: Large barriers are ahead.
Bouquet	True friendship.
Bow and arrow	You doing archery: You are uncertain and worried about your occupation. To see children play: Unanticipated festivities ahead.

If someone points a bow and arrow at you:
Your honor is at stake.
To point and shoot one: Inheritance.
To be hurt by an arrow: You will soon have a
love affair.

Bowl

Made from crystal. It is time to spread your
wings.
To see one: You will receive an invitation.
To hold one: Somebody will try to frighten you.

Bowling

You will come up with a good idea.

Box

To see a large one: You may feel cheated.
To see a pretty gold or silver-colored box: A
symbol that the dreamer will receive an
honorary gift.
An old, bent box: You may encounter old,
unpleasant people or experience other unpleasant things.
To lose a box: You are undecided about
something.
To have a colorful box: Pleasant acquaintances.

Box tree

Seeing this tree in a dream is a symbol of long-
lasting trust amongst a friend or a loved one.

Boys

To see them fight: You may get into trouble
because of your friends, who are involved in
dishonest matters.
To see them play: Money problems may develop
for the married dreamer.

Bracelet

To own one: A sign of future well-being.
To receive one as a gift: This is a symbol of a
secret love affair which you enjoy in your sleep.

Brain

To see one: There is a sad future in store for
you.
To eat: You will soon receive an inheritance.

Bran

You may soon have your own home, or you
may change your address.

Branch

To see a green one: You will accomplish nothing
by talking.
To see one in blossom: If you want to be successful, you will have to try very hard.
To see one without leaves: Things for you are
hopeless right now.

To see a dried-up one: It is necessary to rebuild a more suitable structure.

Branding iron

To see one: Bitter experiences in your love life.

Brandy

To drink it: What once seemed to be a sure thing now requires review.
To see someone else drinking it or to find yourself in a bar: You may make an unfortunate acquaintance and cause harm to befall yourself.

Brass

To see it: Warns of a quarrel with your wife.

Brass band

To see them playing: Good hopes.

Brass founder

To be one: You will marry a wealthy woman from a highly respected family.

Brass utensils

Don't complain about your domestic servant.

Bread

Dark bread: If you are ill, you will soon recover.
To eat white bread: Warns you to be cautious.
To smell fresh bread: Strange visitors.
To see old bread: Trouble is ahead.

Bread basket

To see it empty: Difficult times ahead.
To see a full one: Pleasant times are ahead.

Breakfast

To eat it: The future will be pleasant and harmonious.

Breaking

To cause a break: Accept the loss.

Breast

To see a woman with pretty ones: Pleasant surprises are in store.
To see them small and old-looking: Poverty and sadness.
If a woman sees a man with bare shoulders and chest: Beware of jealousy.
To see a mother feeding a baby: Signifies a happy marriage and homelife.
If someone hits you on your breast: You will experience a frightening event.

Breeze

To hear one: Don't try to make money the easy way; speculative gambles could prove to be unfortunate.

Brewery

To see one: Through your devotion to your work you earn honor and wealth.
To see a brewer at work: You will have luck in lotteries and games.

Briars To see them: Your love life is suffering.
To step on them: You triumph over an opponent.

Brick To see one: The better you know yourself, the more you are likely to succeed.
To see bricks stacked up: Business problems lie ahead.
To see broken bricks: Warns of loss.
To work with bricks: Be patient with the difficult task at hand. If you persevere, towards the end you and others will profit.

Bricklayer To see one working: Hard work will bring its own rewards.

Bride To see her in her attire: Happiness and luck in the future and in marriage.
To sew a wedding dress: You will receive an invitation.
To see or make a bridal veil: This is an omen on illness in the immediate family.
To receive a gift of gold or silver: Happiness in your home.
To receive a gift of pearls, or if the bride is wearing them: Tears.

Bridegroom To be one: A wedding will soon occur.
Best man: A child will soon be born.
To see a bride and groom together: This means that the dreamer will have a happy and harmonious marriage.

Bridal wreath Your husband admires you.

Bridge To see or cross an unknown bridge: You may take a trip across a body of water.
To see a bridge being built: With perseverance your goal will be accomplished.
To see a very old bridge: You may have to cancel your trip.
To stand in front of a collapsed bridge: This means that someone will break a promise.
To see a drawbridge open: You are experiencing some difficulties with your plans.

Bridle To see one: Now you are the winner.
To lose one (if a rider): Accident.

Bright To see something very bright: A good and lucky future.

Brilliant	To dream of diamond-like stones: A good and lucky future ahead.
Brilliantine	Don't be arrogant.
Bristles	To dream about bristles: Be careful: An unfortunate illness may cause your face to become disfigured. You will have to overcome unpleasant situations.
Bronze	To see or own it as a medal: The poor health of a close friend or relative concerns you.
Brooch	To have one: You will find permanent employment.
Brooding heat	You worry unnecessarily.
Brood-hen	To see one: Efficiency and happiness.
Brook	To see a bloody one: Danger of war. To walk through one: You will reach your goal. A clear one: You are contemplating your lifestyle. A rapid one: Misfortune follows you. With fishes in it: Good business dealings. A deep one: You are surrounded by false friends. A muddy one: Fire damage. A dried out one: Troubled and hard times are ahead. Flowing through a house: You will have a good income.
Broom	To turn one upside-down: You will be involved in a fight. To buy one: Bad domestic people. To put one in a corner: You may lose your job. To see a figure riding a broom: Warns of contagious sickness.
Broth	To eat it: If you are sick, recovery. If you are healthy, prosperity.
Brother	To see your brother far away: An unexpected reunion or good news may be expected. To say goodbye to a brother: Happy occurrences.
Brother-in-law	To see him: Unexpected good luck. To talk to him: You are annoyed about problems

which you thought had been solved.
To hear him talk: Don't get too close to your neighbors.

Brothers and sisters
To see them (alive): Pleasant surprises in store.
To see them (dead): Long life.

Brush
If you see a brush. You are upset and worried. Things will not turn out to be as pleasant as you wish them to be.
Someone is talking behind your back.

Brushing
Make sure that you are not overcharged for merchandise.

Bubble
To see them rising from water: This warns you not to grow conceited or unfriendly.
To have bubbles on your body through burns or other mishaps: Trouble amongst friends or relatives.

Bucket
To see one: Honor and dignity.

Bucket-well
To see or work with one: This tells you that it is better to have a small fortune than to have no fortune at all.

Buckle
To have or to see one: You can trust the people you spend the most time with.

Buckwheat
To see a field covered with: Your future will be calm and pleasant.

Bud
To see one: Signifies love, engagement and fulfillment of your wishes.

Buffalo
To see one: You may receive a summons.
To be kicked by one: You are blessed with many children.
To slaughter one: You should fight for your rights.

Building
To see a beautiful big building: You will undertake a new project.
To see a building rise: Poverty and danger are far from your life.
To see an unfinished one: Turbulent days ahead.
To see a building torn down: Clear all handicaps out of your way.
To see a building burning: Your happiness will be clouded.

Building site	To see one: You will be involved in a large project.
Bull	To be kicked by one: A happy love life is in store. To buy one: You will be involved in a dispute. To slaughter one: You may receive sad news. To see bulls in a pasture: You may have a fight to reach your goal.
Bulldog	You will find a guardian or a protector.
Bulldozer	To see one in motion: You have to put a lot of effort into your life.
Bullet	To see one: This is a signal of danger. To be hit by one: Someone near you, or you yourself, must have an operation.
Bullfight	To witness one: You may become ill.
Bullfinch	To see them: Great pleasure.
Bullrush	Unstable luck.
Bun	To buy them: Profit. To eat them: You constantly head in the right direction.
Bundle	To see large bundles: This means high earnings. To pack or to load them: Rewarding occupation. To receive or unpack one: Profitable good news or an unexpected gift. To see a bundle of straw or hay: Some hardship will befall you.
Burden	This could be the most memorable month of the year.
Burglar	To see one: Don't force yourself to be adventurous; you could end up in trouble. To arrest one: Your passion will bring you harm.
Burn	To burn yourself: This is a warning to be cautious and careful. If you try not to act hastily you can avoid accidents. To have burn marks: This means you have triumphed over a dangerous situation. To see a burned forest: The burden will be removed and the tasks will be completed. To burn leaves in the fall: Means great pleasure. To see trash burning: A good omen.

Burning-glass   To use it: You and your spouse are faithful even when far apart.

Burst   To hear: Do not spread falsehoods, as they will bring you unpleasantness.

Bury   To bury a friend: You carry a heavy burden.

Bus   To ride in one: Take better care of yourself.

Bush   To see a green one: You may be invited to attend a happy occasion, such as a wedding.
To see one with pretty flowers: You may have to delay your plans.
If a bush appears dry and droopy: Warns of arguments with neighbors.

Butler   To see one: You will have a good income, but you will have to work hard for it.

Butter   To see fresh butter: Lasting health and some weight gain.
To eat good fresh butter: You are too kind and easy-going and you may have some arguments with your friends.
To eat old butter: Someone is holding a grudge.
To make butter or to see a churn: Your income is good and you may take a trip to the country.
To buy butter: Your eating habits are good, therefore you have good health.

Buttermilk   To drink it: For a farm person, good luck. For others, an early return from a trip.

Butterfly   Your luck won't last forever.

Buttock   To see your own: Insult.
To see a woman's: Hardship.

Button   To tear one off: Your children will cause some trouble.
To see them: People you thought could be trusted turn against you and you are disappointed at their unreliability.

Buzzard   To see one flying: Don't let your job take over your entire life.
To see more than one: Surrounding influences are hostile.
To see one sitting alone: Sadness and worries are imminent.

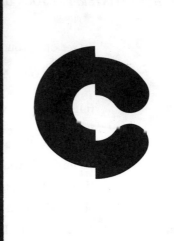

Cab   To see one: You are thinking of opening a business.
To ride in one: A family affair will take place.

Cabbage   To eat one: Influential people will not lift a finger to help you.

Cabin   Discuss ways in which you can pull close together with your loved ones.

Cabinet   To buy one: Your lifestyle will improve.

Cabinet-maker   You will take a big step ahead.

Cable   To see: Good news.

Cablegram   To receive one: Do not act rashly.

Cable-car   For the next fews days you will be successful in gambling.

Cachou   To have some in your hand: Light sickness.

Cackle   To hear poultry cackle: You are situated quite well.

Cadaver   To see a cremation: Luck will occur very soon.

Cafe   To see or sit in a cafe: You have spent your time unproductively.

Cage   To see one: You will find professional advice extremely helpful.

Cake   To see one: A festive celebration.
To bake one: Sometimes, a small gift could bring you good friendship.
To eat a piece: Sickness may appear.

Calamus   To pick: Spending for pleasure must be kept moderate.

Calendar   To see one: A pleasant surprise.
To hold one: You may someday marry a widow or a widower.

Calculate   You are losing an inheritance.

Calf   To see one being slaughtered: Workers may have differences with their superiors.
To see them in a pasture: Watch what you say to people who tend to become upset easily.

Call   To call someone: Endure sickness.

To hear somebody else: Keep in touch with influential people whose support is valuable to you.

Calumniated   To be: Love life could distort true picture.

Camarilla   To see them around you: You are put under pressure by surrounding enemies.

Cambric   To dream about this cloth means: You will be very happy with a present received from a dear person.

Camels   To see one: You will receive an invitation.
To see a caravan of camels: Your life will be full of work.

Camera   To handle one: Someone is spying on you.

Camp   Your distress will change soon.

Canal   The day should be used for rest and relaxation.

Canary   To see one: It is better that you are discreet now; many people do not want your advice.
To hear him sing: Don't be too trusting.
To see a stuffed one: You find out that one of your friends is dishonest.
To see a dead one: Your own mistake will cause a loss.
To see one escape: Your love is given gratuitously.
To see one chased by a cat: One of your neighbors is not candid with you.

Cancan   To do the dance or see others doing: Happy times are ahead.

Candidate   To see or speak to one: This is a favorable day for spending money.

Candle   To see one: Grief and distress.
To see a lighted one: Luck is on your doorstep, but don't be impatient.
To see many: One of your acquaintances is very ill and will die.
To see one being extinguished: Your wishes won't come true.
To see a long one: You will live a long life.

Candlestick   Made of china: Have you ever thought of doing volunteer work to help others?

With a lighted candle: If you have an innovative idea or a product to sell, this is the time to make your pitch.

Candy To eat: Be aware of tricks.

Cane To be hit with one: Your future is uncertain.
To have one: Action replaces lethargy.
To find one: Show them that you are courageous, otherwise they will look down upon you.

Cannon To see one: It is necessary to drive carefully.
To see one in action: A friend tells you a distasteful story.
To hear one: Look out for false flatterers.

Cannon ball Prove to them that you can keep your mouth shut when you have to - don't divulge secrets.

Canoe To see one: Secret affairs should be avoided.
To be in one: Don't put yourself in a dangerous situation.

Canopy To see one: Your work will be recognized and appreciated.

Canyon Exciting changes occur.

Cap To see an old one: There is success and dignity after a long time without.
To see a new one: Failure in business.
To wear one: The day is best put to use for obtaining knowledge and for self-improvement.

Cape To wear one: A happy and exciting time for romance.

Capriccio To hear the music: Your moodiness irritates others.

Captain To see or be one: You have a long and happy life ahead.

Captivity To be in: Good things will happen.
People far away may soon come home.

Capuchin monk To see them: Creative projects offer opportunities for increasing their values.

Car Profit is on the way.

Caravan To see one: You overcome all barriers.

Carcass
A decomposed human means overall grief and mourning.
Death or other misfortune may occur.
*If the body is only dead and not yet decayed, the meaning differs and will be explained under corpse and individual animals.

Cardboard
To see: Someone will betray you.

Cardinal
To see one: Satisfaction.

Cards
To play: You may have to struggle in order to reach your goal.

Care
You are basically a good person, although occasionally you tend to be a bit greedy.

Caress
Good outlook for success.

Carmen
To sing the opera or attend the play: A wedding will take place.

Carnation
To pick one: Pleasure and delight are on the way.

Carnival
Look out for pickpockets.

Carp
To eat one: Money troubles in the near future.
To catch one: Try to have more contact with your relatives.

Carpenter
You will reach your goal shortly.

Carpet
To buy one: Friends will visit you.

Carré
To build a space like that: You will victoriously triumph over your opponent.

Carriage
To sit in one: Luck and honor.
To see one with horses: Happiness.
To see one with a donkey: A dull social gathering.

Carrier
To see one: An agreement or a contract can be renegotiated.

Carrots
To harvest them: You have to endure a lot of things.

Cartouche
To see or hold one: Your most difficult undertakings will be successful.

Case
To see one: It would be far better for your relationships if you would be less hot-tempered and a little bit calmer.

Cash-box   To work with one: You may find it necessary to devote more time to domestic affairs.

Casting   Casting of a statue of a field-marshall or a general: Beware of danger.

Castle   You may soon go on a trip.
                      To be inside one: Anxiety and worries.
                      To find it locked: You will witness something unusual.
                      To see a castle gate open: Watch out - unknown danger.
                      To see a ruined castle: A betrayed friendship.
                      To see a vine-covered castle: It could be the start of something very big.

Catapult   To see one: Watch the traffic.

Cataract   Gossiping.

Catch   Somebody: It will take time to get rid of an importunate person.
                      To catch something: Something pleasurable will excite you.

Catching   Catching a thief: Somebody in your family is talking evil of you.

Catechism   To read one: Communications received from one who was out of sight.

Caterpillar   To see them: Sickness.
                      To catch them: Respect.
                      To see damage done by caterpillars on a tree: Profit and victory.

Cathedral   To see one: You will find comfort.
                      To be inside one: An omen to make you aware of your feelings.
                      To see a canon: You may receive false information.

Cats   To play with one: One of your closest friends is revealed to be a traitor.
                      To be scratched by one: Take care of your belongings at home.

Cattle   To see them: Excitement in business affairs.

Cavalier   To meet one: A big loss is possible.

Cave   To enter one: There is a trap set for you, but you don't see it.

Caviar	To eat it: You may be involved in an accident - be cautious.
Cedars	To see pretty and tall trees: You will reach your goal, have inner peace and a happy, honorable future.
Celery	To eat: Aid comes discreetly.
Cellar	To be in one: Have more patience with your children.
Cellist	To see yourself as a cellist: You will enter the aristocratic ranks of society.
Cemetery	To see one: Your proposition will fail. To walk in: Try to spend more time with your loved ones. To pass by one: A quiet and peaceful retirement is in the future.
Ceremonial opening	Creative work holds some possibility of continued success.
Cession	To give up: You may plan to set up a testament.
Chaff	Wealth and honor in your future.
Chains	To see them: Your luck is uncertain, if you go a false way.
Chair	To sit in one: One day you will hold high office.
Chairman	To see him: Pay more attention to the people working with you. To speak to him: The next time you will be successful in gambling.
Challenge	To challenge someone to a duel: Disagreements and misunderstandings.
Chamber	To see one: You will soon move to a different state. To be in one: Do what you can to make your own four walls harmonious.
Chamber-maid	To see one: Arguments could develop with relatives.
Chambray	To work with: Visitors will arrive.
Chamois	To see them: You will fulfill your plans ahead of time.
Champagne	To drink it yourself: You may commit a breach of faith.

To see others drink it: This is telling you be aware of friends or lovers. The times you spend with them are uncertain.
Overall, to dream about champagne means: Happiness is only for a short time.

Chandelier

To see one: A social evening that you have arranged may have to be postponed.
To see a lighted one: Good success in business.
To buy one: You may attain a better position.

Chansonette

To be one: Your lifestyle is very loose.

Chaplain

Speak to one: Professional advice is especially important.

Chapel

To pray in: You find comfort in your grief.

Charcoal

To see it glow: Time is better for selling than for buying.
To be extinguished: Lovers grief troubles you.

Charitable

To be: It reveals well being.

Charity

To organize one or give to a charity: You will find helpful people.

Charlatan

To see one: Someone tries to seduce you.
Speak to one: Somebody likes to cheat on you.

Charnel-house

Death and danger.

Charter

To charter a boat or go sailing on a cruise: Your undertaking will be fruitful.

Chased

To be: Overcome your tendency to be impatient where basic procedures are concerned.

Chat

You have the best intentions, nevertheless, you will be misunderstood.

Cheeks

Healthy and red cheeks: Happiness and well being.
Pale ones: Distress.
Covered with make up: Be aware if you cheat, or if you intend to mislead someone.
To hit someone's cheeks: A dispute is ahead.
To get hit: A happy surprise.
To see one bloody or scratched: You find yourself in a troublesome situation caused by inconsiderate behavior.

Cheese	To eat: Real estate transactions are likely to produce some good luck. Spoiled: Sickness.
Chef	To see one: You get another boss. Talk to one: Your income will increase. To be one: Unpleasant news.
Chemisette	To see or wear one: Your future will be difficult.
Chemist	People try to be good to you.
Cherries	To eat them: Luck is on your doorstep but don't be impatient.
Cherry tree	To see one: A nice wedding is coming up. To see in blossom: You are yearning for far away places, but better stay home. The other shore always seems greener.
Cherub	To see one: You can put full trust in happiness.
Chess	To play it: Be aware of swindlers.
Chestnut tree	To see one: Prosperous future. To eat chestnuts: Decisions are favorable.
Chicken	To see them: Unpleasant situation. To see a hen roast: A lucky homelife.
Chignon	To wear one: You take the truth very lightly.
Child	To see a well-behaved one: You will meet someone and one day this person will be a good friend to you. To have one: Don't be overly optimistic - this can lead to extravagance.
Childbed	Beware of empty promises.
Children	To play with them: The best things in life cost nothing. Do not overlook them.
Child's play	To see: This easy-going time gives you the chance to deal with personal issues.
Chimes	You will receive and be honored with a distinctive medal.
Chimney	People are unfair to you.

Chimney sweep	To see one: You will be cleared of suspicion. To meet one: Luck in lottery. To talk to him: Unexpected luck will befall you.
Chinese	To see or talk with a Chinese person: Through moderation and eagerness you will achieve your goal.
Chinin	To dream about it: The time ahead will be unsettled.
Chive	To eat: Don't lose your keys.
Chlor	To smell chlor: Your health will improve.
Chloroform	Someone tries to anaesthetize you with it: You will venture into some pleasant things.
Chocolate	To eat it: You are alive and kicking - let the world know it.
Choir	To hear one: A loving warning sign to search within yourself and become a more understanding person. To be a member of one: Lack of enthusiasm for an enterprising venture. To see one: Wealth at home.
Chop off	Chop off something: Missing a prize winning.
Chopping block	To work on one: You have to bear a worrisome and unpleasant situation.
Chorale	To hear: For single people; Marriage. For married people: Faithful spouse.
Christ	To see Him: You find comfort in your sadness. To see Him on the cross: You can fall into vicious corruption. To hear Him talk: Cheerful times. To pray to Him: You are devoted to God.
Christmas	To celebrate: Your hopes could become a reality as a result of something that may happen today or tomorrow.
Christmas gift	Because of your assiduity you have a lot of good helpful friends.
Christmas tree	To see this tree in your dream: It allows you to foresee an unexpected big and happy surprise, which may be a beautiful gift or an unexpected reunion with a loved person.

	To buy one: A kind deed will win you a new admirer.
Church	To go into one: Improvement in everything. To see one on fire: Danger of war.
Church-bell	To hear them: One of your main wishes will be fulfilled.
Church festival	Do not embarrass your family.
Church going	To see people go to church: Your wish will not come true.
Cider	To drink it: You are a slave to your passion.
Cigar	To see somebody smoke one: A relative will call and remind you of a past favor. To smoke one yourself: You will locate an item that had been misplaced.
Circle	To see one: Try to get rid of some of your bad habits.
City	A big one: Delight and adventure. A small one: Some of your wishes require revision.
Clarinet	To hear one: The advice of friends should not be followed.
Clasp	Take care of evil people.
Clay	To see it: You cannot count on an increase in salary. To work with wet clay: Concentrate more on business activities, less on the personal side of your life.
Clay-pit	You will retire as a rich person.
Cleaning	People love to have parties at your place.
Clearing	A table by yourself: Upset stomach. To watch another clearing it: Warning to be thrifty.
Clergyman	To see one: You can count on an unexpected reputation. To hear him preach: Prosperity in the future.
Clerk	To see one: Sad expectations for the next while.
Climb	Up on a tree: Not a happy day for romance, but

good for creative work.
To see someone climb up one: Honesty is always life's best policy.

Clock   To wind one up: Play it safe where a financial venture is concerned.

Clothes   Old ones: Your work pays less money.

Clouds   To see bright ones: A disaster will pass you by.
To see dark ones: Your lifestyle will improve.
To see fast moving ones: You will lose something and gain something also.
To see irregular ones: You are of good character.
To see a cloudburst: You have to overcome a hazardous situation.
To see them in the sunset: Chance to win at gambling.
To see them very high in the sky: Through hard work it is possible that you may become wealthy.

Clover-leaf   To see or have one: Help a friend who is in trouble.

Clown   To see one: Be aware - you are being used to the utmost.

Club   To join one: You will receive a court summons.

Coach   To see one: You will be free of trouble if you don't change your goal.

Coals   To buy some: Any contacts that can be made with professional people are important.
To handle coal: You may enter a lifelong job with good income, but you will never become wealthy.

Coal-mine   To be in one: You could easily be a millionaire, but you are too lazy.

Coal-stove   To see one: Differences can easily develop with co-workers which can interfere with work.

Coat   To wear a new one: Your worries will soon be over.
To lose one: Try to avoid slipping into poverty.
To wear a ragged one: You will find sympathy.
To take one off: You will be disgraced.
Wear a too large one: Worries and headaches.
To see someone dressed in a coat: Misrepresentation.

Coat of arms	To see them: Your life is in danger.
Coax	You will be disappointed in your hopes.
Cock	To see him lay eggs: A rich inheritance and good luck. To see a pretty one: You will be cherished and loved by the other sex. To hear him crowing: You will receive unpleasant news. To see a cock-fight: Unpleasantness in business or marriage.
Cockatoo	To see one: Your melancholy for far away places will become a reality.
Cod-liver oil	To smell or drink it: Worry can be reduced if you are more tactful.
Coffee	To make it: Family expenses may be too high. To drink: Influential people may be difficult.
Coffee-grinder	To handle one: You will hear bad news.
Coffee-pot	To smash one: For single people: Don't lose your patience. For married people: You cannot buy happiness with money.
Coffee-shop	A next of kin will be involved in an accident.
Coffin	To see one means for sick people: Get well. For healthy people: A long life. To lie in it: Unsteady luck.
Cohabitation	With a lover: Fulfillment of the wish with this person.
Coins	To see small coins: In your lifetime you will accumulate wealth and security. To see silver coins: Time is on your side.
Colander	To use one: You won't receive love in return.
Cold	To have one: Be prepared to accept additional responsibilities.
Collapse	Of a building: This project is not as good as you thought, but you are full of ideas. Try something new.
Collection	Of beetles: A shameful and a dishonorable death. Of plants: Happiness and grief at the same time.
Collection box	Misery and distress is ahead of you.

Colonnade	To see one: Hours of pleasure in sight.
Colt	To see them in a pasture: Strive for greater independence.
Comb	To buy one: Differences with your brother or sister. To comb yourself: You receive very important mail.
Combat	To see: Struggle for a living; grief about your children.
Comedy	To see one: A forecast of successful business.
Comet	To see one: Bad times and accidents are possible.
Comfort	Other people: Someone attempts to burden you with unnecessary problems.
Command	To order someone around: Trouble and ill humor. Or you may get a job in which you have authority.
Communicate	Transactions should be postponed.
Community	To find yourself in one: You volunteer for the welfare of others.
Companion	To be with a fellow: Cheerfulness and happiness.
Compass	To see one: Double-check time tables and travel arrangements.
Complaint	To hear one: Success and gain.
Composition-book	To write in one: Expected news will arrive. Turning pages in a book: You will meet with friends from the past. To tear a book: Hurt feelings. To hold one in your hand: Disagreement between relatives.
Comptoir	To work in: You will make good business.
Conceited	To be: Your children may ask you for a favor. Don't deny them.
Concert	To hear one: You are searching for a different lifestyle. With the help of others your yearning will become true.
Condemned	To be: Don't be tempted.

	To see condemned people: You will escape danger.
Cone	Do not push your luck away.
Confectionery	To be in one: Some unexpected good fortune is possible through new ideas.
Confession	Talk to the father confessor. Relieving pain from your trouble. To see a father confessor: You are committing a sin.
Confirmation	A gain in lottery.
Congratulate	Your friends are not dependable.
Congress	To attend: Business may clash with the personal side of your life.
Connection	To get: Improve security measures.
Conquer	Temporary success.
Consolation	To get: You get help from people you never thought of.
Conspiracy	Minor ailments could require special attention.
Constable	To see one: Unnecessary involvement.
Constellation	To see them: People who recently opposed you will now begin to see the wisdom of your plans.
Construction	A structure half finished: Finish your undertaking with passion and ambition. A complete beautiful one: Your big plan will be a great success. An old and ugly one: Disappointed hopes and trouble. To see one collapse: A major accident which can involve you or your family. To build one yourself: Your undertaking will be fruitless. To see others build one: You have friends that you can count on.
Container	Made of earthenware: If you take precautions you can prevent loss. Made out of iron: Be economical. Made out of porcelain: Things are looking good in the future.

Contempt	To be: Someday you will discover a treasure.
Contract	To sign one: You are in the mood to spend a lot of money. Think twice.
Contribution	To pay: Someone will introduce you to a friend.
Cookies	To buy: Means interruption in some anticipated pleasure.
Cooper	To see him involved with his work: Messages should be given particular attention as they may contain incorrect details.
Cooperator	To see a co-worker: New contacts can be useful.
Copper	To see: Keep your temper, even though you feel you are being baited.
Copy	To make some: There will be a big change in your life.
Copying-pencil	To buy: You will meet an unexpected acquaintance.
Copying-press	This day can be useful for obtaining information that can be helpful to speculative ventures.
Coral	You get quick good results from yesterday's activities.
Cordon	To see guards enclosing an area: You may slip into an unpleasant situation.
Corn	To harvest corn: Well-being through continuing ambition. To sell corn: You will be blessed with many children. To buy corn: A useful agreement may be negotiated.
Corn (on the foot)	To have: A friend is moving away.
Corpse	To see one: A long and healthy life. To see more than one: Let justice run its course; do not try to change it. To see one in a casket: Be prepared to have visitors who will stay a long time.
Corpulent	To see yourself corpulent: There will be an increase in your belongings.
Correct	To be: An inconsiderate word starts a big quarrel.

Cotillion	To see or watch a dance: You will fall in love.
Cottage	To see one: Happiness and satisfaction with what you have. To be at one: Accidentally, you will find a missing friend.
Cottage cheese	To eat: Your honesty will cause you to acquire enemies.
Cotton	To have cotton garments: Winnings. To see a cotton field: Much happiness. To buy cotton garments: Loss of money.
Cough	To be coughing: You will receive a short and negative answer.
Count	See yourself counting: You can obtain the cooperation of influential people which can be especially important to creative enterprises.
Counterfeit money	To have: You are suspicious for no reason. To see: Don't buy anything which you cannot afford. To make it: Be aware of an accident.
Counterpane	To see one: The unpleasant thing which bothers you will not surface.
Country	To see one devastated: Your future is uncertain.
Country house	To see one: Real estate is not always as valuable as you think.
Coupe	To sit in one: Very pleasant experience.
Couplet	To hear one: You will fall into a conflict.
Coupon	To clip them: Your friends and family are devoted to you.
Courier	To see one: Trips or visits are not likely to produce good results.
Court	To be summoned: Someone is out to harm your reputation. To stand in front of a judge: Your feelings will be hurt. To see a court bailiff or to hear him talking: Be alert of bad people in business. You will get the short end of the stick.
Courteous	To be: Unhappy news may be expected.

Cousin

To dream about a cousin: You may have a hidden affair.
To be with one: You will spread rumors.

Cowl

To wear one: A struggle could come to a successful close today.

Cow barn

To see one: Your wealth is increasing.

Cows

To milk them: Don't wait for an inheritance.
To see black ones: Sick people will recover.
To see them waiting for milking: You will benefit from co-workers.

Crabs

To see them: You are able to make plans for the future quite successfully.
To catch them: Friends will make good company.

Cradle

To see one: What appears abstract can actually serve as a reliable guide.

Cranberries

To eat: You will get an invitation.

Crane

To see or to hear them: Try to understand your children and give them a break.

Crank

To turn on: If you do something risky, think carefully of the long term consequences.

Crates

To see empty ones: You will meet unpleasant people and you will have no chance to avoid them in the future.
To see them full of something: You will receive a nice gift.

Crayon

To write with: You uncover a fraud.

Cream

To make whipped cream: Set your own pace in order to remain healthy.
To buy: With your own power you survive best.
To drink: Your health is perfect.
To see: Do not demand too much from your destiny.

Creditor

Calling on you: You will overcome problems with your enemies.

Creeps

To see them: Your love will be returned to you.

Crew

Impending luck.

Crickets

To see or hear them: You are freed from suspicion.

For sick people: Delayed recovery.

Crinoline   You are losing something nice.

Cripple   To see one: It is a bad omen.
To talk to one: It is a good omen.

Croak   To hear something: You and your partner are in total accord Keep it that way.

Crockery   To see: Some arguments between family members.
To break up dishes: You are going to be single and unable to hold on to friends.

Croquet   To play this game or see it being played: You will get an invitation to go to a dance.

Cross   To see one: Your faith moves mountains.
To see one covered up: Be thankful for your health.

Crossbar   You will be aware of a secret.

Cross-bow   To use one: Fear and distress.
To break one: Good future.

Cross examination   Take nothing for granted where legal affairs are concerned.

Crossroads   To see: There will soon be a change in your life.

Crow   To see them: An enemy will try to do you some harm.
To hear them cawing: You will receive an obituary notice.
To see them fly around a house: A life will end there.

Crowd   To see a large one: Business will be profitable.
To be in one: Arguments and trouble.

Crowned heads   To see them: Your happiness is on the on and off swing.
To see yourself crowned: Your arrogant behavior must come to an end.

Crucible   Great pleasure will come soon.

Crucifix   Disappointed hopes.

Crude oil   To buy it: You gain greater popularity by being more outspoken.
To use it: This year you will travel a lot.

Cruise   To be on one: Arguments can develop with friends over money.
                        To plan one: Don't expose yourself to danger.

Crush   Find somebody you can talk to. You really have need for a close friend right now.

Crutches   To see them: Some effort should be made to complete long delayed affairs.
                        To walk with them: Wealth and success.

Cry   During sleep: Delight and pleasure.
                        To see someone cry: Do not trouble yourself about other peoples concerns.

Crystal   To see: It will be very useful to think about your old age security.

Cuckoo   To see one: Means luck and profit.
                        To hear one: Means a long life.

Cucumber   To eat them: You are not discreet in dispatching your private business.
                        To plant cucumber seeds: Sudden events can cause severe loss.

Cudgel   You will be paralysed with fear.

Cuff-links   A trouble will fade away.

Cuffs   To dream about them: Don't be arrogant.

Cultivation of rice Unexpected actions with impulsive people can cause upsets with speculative ventures.

Cunning   To seem: Take it easy if you are seeking pleasure and entertainment away from home.

Cup   A lady friend will call on you.

Curiosity   Devote more time to planning for your future.

Curls   To have: Don't change your mind on a very important matter.
                        To cut them off: Make more plans about your future; forget troubles from yesterday.

Curling iron   To use one: Bitter experience in your love-life.

Curse   Unscrupulous people talk about your secret.

Curtain   To hang them up: You are hiding something.

Curtsy   To do: Your effort to obtain a better position

	and more money may not bring immediate results.
Cushion	To see one: Sad days ahead of you.
Cut	A happy reunion with a loved one.
Cylinder	To see one: In general a very good omen.
Cypress	To see them: You can accomplish more at home than at your place of employment today.

Dachshund	To play with one: Don't delay your proposals. If you do, you could be too late.
Dagger	To have one: Don't push yourself into a dangerous situation. To be injured by one: Accept an unexpected invitation. It could prove to be advantageous for you. To fight with one: Don't give up - the law is on your side.
Dainties	Annoyance at home.
Dam	To see one: You gain access to confidential information.
Damask	Through sensual pleasures you will be harmed.
Dance	To see people dancing: Luck in love. If you are dancing: Contact with people who work in the background could help you to solve a puzzle.
Danger	To be in: You find that you need to calm down.
Darkness	To see: War and bad times are imminent. To be in: Controversies with friends; be careful.
Date	To see a date on a calendar: You will be occupied with some important matters.
Date palm	To have one: You will hold a financial trump card.
Dates	To eat dates: For a man means: You will be loved by a woman. For a lady means: You will have more than one admirer. To be given a gift of dates: Your relatives are pleasant, however, they are not especially important to your plans.
Daughter	To have one: It is not wise to rely on support from influential people. If she is talking to you: You receive good advice.
Daughter-in-law	To see her: People have different opinions about you.
Day laborer	Your social life accelerates. Make plans for the weekend.
Dead	To be: Good health. To see yourself: Pleasurable life. To dig up a corpse: Some danger in sight.

To be with dead people: It is a good sign.
To kiss a deceased person: Your hopes and wishes will be fulfilled.

Deaf   To be: You will regret something.

Dean   To see or talk to a dean: You will be thrown into despair by the miscarriage of a plan, which originally promised good fortune.

Death sentence   To hear your own: Your luck will stay, because you took good care of everything.
To read one: An omen of bad reputation.

Debris   To see: Sometime in the future will be a prosperous life.

Debtor   To meet one: Watch out for a swindler.

Debts   To make them: Welcome visitors to your home. They will bear good news.
To pay them: Do not withdraw your savings for a business investment.
To pay them for somebody else: You, who is usually quiet, will speak up in a bold manner.

Debut   To see a first appearance: Your work will be successful.

Decapitated   Fearful and disagreeable things enter your life.

Decimal-scale   To see this scale: Means that creative work will produce good results.

Deck   To be on a deck: Your undertakings will be fruitful.

Declaim   To declaim something: You may experience preferential treatment.

Decorate   To have decoration done: Lack of own opinion.
To do your own: You may have an unfair advantage.

Deer   To see them: Friends will visit you.
To eat deer meat: Success and wealth.
To feed them: You are a sure victor over your opponent.

Defect   To find or spot a defect: You will meet some untidy, disorderly people.

Deficit   To have one: You may become involved in a court matter.

Defile   To watch a march in line: A peaceful settlement
                     of differences.

Degraded   To be degraded: This means that knowing
                     yourself is the key to being able to predict and
                     understand your own future.

Delegate   To become one: Don't make a fool of yourself.

Delicatessen   To see or eat in one: Check costs. Your mate's
                     taste may be too extravagant for your budget.

Delighted   To be: Your burden will be removed and your
                     cash flow resumes.
                     Your career progresses in the right direction.
                     To see someone else: A member of the opposite
                     sex will be of help in acquiring an important
                     contact.

Delinquent   To dream about delinquency: You probably
                     have debts on your mind which must be repaid.

Delirious   To be in this state: You may fall into the hands
                     of a swindler.

Deluded   To be: You will be disgraced because you com-
                     mitted a sin.

Demi monde   To see: Be more honest with your friends.

Democracy   You will have great delight in bringing a new
                     enterprise to completion.

Demonstration   To see one: Someone who instigates legal action
                     may have hidden motives. Get expert advice
                     before you respond.
                     To be involved in one: There may be some dif-
                     ficulties at work.

Denounce   Someone is denouncing you: Everything you do
                     is being watched.

Dentist   To see him at work: Your success depends upon
                     your ability to cope with opposition.
                     To have an appointment with one: Enemies are
                     endeavoring to take possession of your property
                     by foul means.

Denude   Yourself: Try to have more confidence in
                     yourself. Also, you will reveal a secret.
                     Somebody else: A member of the opposite sex
                     will ask for a definite commitment.

Departure
There will be a change in the
likely a change for the better

Deported
To be deported: You fall int
tion.

Depot
To see one: Do not complain about y~
You have no reason to.

Depressed
Feeling depressed: You should not begin any
new projects.

Deprive
You deprive someone: Your gain is obtained
through improper actions.
Someone is depriving you: The mail you receive
may contain news which is difficult to handle.

Desert
To live in one: Your yearnings will not allow you
any peace.
To see one: You have to leave your present
place.
To see one with camels: Empathize with poor
people. Not everyone is as fortunate as you are.
To die of thirst in a desert: Someone is jealous of
your luck. Try to make him your friend.

Deserter
To see or talk to one: You must overcome a
temptation.

Desperation
Fortune will smile upon you.

Despot
To be despotic: The plans you have begun will
end happily.

Detective
To talk to one: Original ideas should be discussed with only those individuals who are directly
involved with putting them into order.
To be a detective: Your friends are un-
cooperative.

Detonation
To hear one: You will receive a surprising
message.

Devil
To see him: Postpone the start of new projects
and/or the signing of legal documents.
To talk to him: Save your eloquence for matters
of principle.
To hear him: You may be overwhelmed by
slander and gossip.

Devout
To be: You will look to the future with a very
calm mind.

	To see it on plants: Your dreams will be fulfilled. To see it on trees: A very good time is ahead of you.
Diadem	To buy one: Spending on luxury items should be postponed. To wear one: Don't be lavish. To see one: A pleasant reconciliation for you after a serious disagreement.
Diamond	To find one: Your love will be returned. To see one shine: Be aware of deception and mild illness. To receive one as a gift: You will be blessed with true friendship. To wear one: Your intellectual interests bring you into contact with individuals who share your concerns.
Diapers	To see them: Try to make life a bit easier for your spouse.
Diarrhea	To have: Numerous opportunities become available.
Dice	To see them: Your advisor may be misinformed. To play with them: A wish will be fulfilled.
Dictate	To dictate a letter: You may have a business meeting that requires outside help.
Dig for treasure	To dream about: Someone will try to trick you. To see yourself doing: Your undertaking will be recognized.
Dike	To walk on one: A very beneficial change is about to occur. To see a dike break: You have to be cautious and protect yourself. To see one: A trip may not produce good results.
Dilettante	To find yourself as one: You may have trouble with someone who holds you in confidence.
Dinner	To be invited to: Turbulent days coming up.
Director	To see one: Correspondence can produce useful information.
Directory	You are looking in and turning the pages of one: A family affair will take place.

	To read one: Minor annoyances can cause impatience.
Dirt	To wade in: Favorable agreements can be reached. To be dirty: Foul talking behind your back. To see dirt: Unexpected good fortune.
Disaster	To dream about one: It is because of your own stupidity that you cannot reach your goal.
Discolor	Ideas can be transformed into viable concepts.
Discovery	To hide: Your apprehension will fade. To make one: A wish comes true in an unusual manner.
Discussion	To have one with a friend: There will soon be a reconciliation.
Dishonor	To be dishonorable: Avoid becoming the middle person in a family dispute. To feel: Be mature enough to avoid compounding an error.
Disinherit	A death in your family.
Displeasure	To feel: You make peace with an enemy.
Dispute	To have one: Through a lawsuit, an agreement will be reached.
Distinction medal	To wear one: Unpleasant news. To be decorated: Your knowledge will be honored.
Ditch	To see a ditch with a culvert: Beware of corruption. A deep counter scarp: Danger and unhappiness.
Divan	To sit on one: Be tolerant and patient to avert quarrels with neighbors.
Dive	Yourself: Unnecessary spending and speculation may cause a problem.
Divine service	To be present at one: You will enter a prosperous employment.
Divining-rod	To see one: What had previously been out of reach now becomes available. To have one: People are interested in your actions.

Divorce

To get through one: Friction surrounds you.

Doctor

To see one: Later you will regret your unpredictable lifestyle.

To speak to one: Humble hopes will enter your heart.

To see one operating: There will soon be recovery from sickness.

Document

To see one: Examine your testament.

To have one: Credit you have received is overdue; avoid paying high interest.

To receive one: Your greediness is inexcusable.

To read one: Most likely, you will become involved in a lawsuit.

To open one: Inheritance.

Dogs

To see them: You will have true friends.

To hear one bark: You are not welcome at one of your neighbors' homes.

To see one sick: You should arrange to see your doctor for a check-up.

To chase one: You may get into danger.

To play with them: Luck in affairs of business.

To see hunting dogs: Friends with whom you had differed will reunite.

If they are biting you: Inheritance causes family problems.

To dream of a large one: You have good and helpful friends surrounding you.

If they are biting each other: Although you will be taken advantage of, in the end everything will work out.

Doll

To see a doll in your dream: This means that you have a happy home.

Dollar

To find one: Tread lightly today or you could set off some fireworks.

To see one made of gold: Your marriage will be a singularly happy one.

Dolphin

To see them swim: Affection and honor.

To see them play: Misfortune.

Domino

Your current situation is unstable.

Donation

To receive one: The sincerity of your sympathy is doubted by others.

Donkey

To see a loaded one: Slowly but surely you will reach your goal.

To buy one: You find practical uses for what had been considered abstract concepts.

Donor

To see one giving blood: You will have honest support.
To be a donor: Don't change jobs.

Door

To see one: A valid business opportunity comes into focus.
To open one: You receive additional recognition with a promise of financial reward.
To see a closed one: If you try hard enough to get the position you want, you will be successful.
To go through one: Someone's negative comments may be nothing but a bid for attention.

Doormat

Focus on travel plans, education and fulfillment of your aspirations.

Dough

To make it: You will get into a dispute with a friend.

Downpour

To be in one: Your children treat you improperly.
To see one: Take advantage of your good ideas.

Down quilt

To see yourself sleeping on a quilt: Slow down and give yourself a rest. You are becoming exhausted.
To see a lot of down feathers: Some strain on your resources seems inevitable.

Downward

To fall: It would be unwise to use your savings for new investments.

Dowry

You will find that the cooperation of your spouse or partner is invaluable when carrying out work around the house.

Draft

Somebody who gives you orders is not more cunning, he is just impudent - restrain yourself.

Drag chain

You would not be feeling so nervous if your abilities were under professional scrutiny.

Dragon

To see one: You may come into contact with obnoxious people.
To be scared of a dragon: This is not the time to take on new commitments.

Dragoon

To see them in uniform: Don't let too many people know about your future plans.
To be one: Don't boast about a recent success.

	To talk to him: It will be better if you control your temper.
Drama	To go to a theater: News of a loved one you have not seen for a while makes you feel more secure.
Draught-board	To play this game: Do not allow your high spirits to affect your home life.
Draw	To draw a sketch: New opportunities exist. Fresh contacts prove to be stimulating and past errors can be erased.
Drawer	To look into one: Your efforts are wasted.
Drawing	To witness one: It would be fruitful if you would concentrate more on your business.
Drawing-board	Put more effort into your work. Your responsibilities are big.
Dress	To see one: Be satisfied with your life and don't hesitate to help other people. To take one off: You will lose a girl friend. To see a blue one: True love from your spouse. To see one burn: You will stand accused. To see a yellow one: Falseness and jealousy among your friends. To see a green one: Your hopes will come true. To iron one: Some of your relatives may come to visit. To see a nice one: You may get pregnant. To see a black one: Your lover will leave you. To clean one: You should live a more proper life. To wear a white one: You will get married within the next year. To see a torn one: An importunated person will trouble you.
Dressmaking	To work as one: Your business is a big success.
Drill	To see someone work with one: A request that you make for time off work will not be granted.
Drink	Clear water: You will be released from a burden. Out of a cup: You will learn what harshness means to you.
Drinker	Make necessary adjustments to your lifestyle.
Drive	In your own car: You will sustain a loss, but it will be your own fault.

Dromedary	To see them in a zoo: In spite of worries and hard work, your life is happy. To see a caravan of them: Be careful - someone would like to hurt you.
Drop	To see them drip: Be aware of a loss.
Drowned	To become: Spend more time with your family. They all love you very much.
Drum	To hear one: Buy property for investment purposes.
Drummer	To see one: You hear about news which is very interesting to you.
Drunk	To be intoxicated or to see others: A health problem may interrupt your schedule again.
Drunkard	To talk to him: Get rid of your stubbornness. To drink with him: Unless you change your lifestyle, you will not reach your goal.
Dry	To dry your hair: A member of the family may fall ill.
Ducat	To hear them clink: Do not try to contact influential people. To wear them on a necklace: For married people, money differences could arise.
Duck	To catch one: Take better care of your complicated business. To eat one: You can be proud of your success. To pluck feathers: Be careful; a small matter could get you into big trouble. To see them in the water: A compliment could make you blush with pride.
Duel	To see one: You will have finished your project soon, and lucky you, you will find it to be the greatest success of your life. To be involved in one: Do not go pleasure-seeking today.
Dumplings	To make them: Preparing more nutritious food will be better and healthier for your family. To eat them: Watch your weight.
Dungeon	To see or to be in one: Bad business or even a bankruptcy.

Dust   To see it: Your dynamic qualities attract the opposite sex.

Dwelling house   To see one: A wrong prototype leads you in a false direction.

Dynamite   To see or to work with it: Beware of a dangerous situation.

Eagle

To see one ascend: An important document should be thoroughly scrutinized before it is signed.
To see one in front of you: Your expectation is nearly fulfilled.
To shoot or see one dying: Displeasure and irritation.
To see a black one flying with his prey: A secret transaction may prove to be valuable.
To catch one: Triumph over an enemy.
If he is tied down and in captivity: A useful agreement can be reached with your partner or spouse.
To own one: Good luck in speculation.
If one is sitting on your head: Disgrace.
For a woman to see one flying over the house: You will marry a respectable man.

Earl

To be a count: You are losing the respect of others.

Earrings

To find one: Soon you will make a good deal.
To buy them: Don't be so idle.
To lose one: Loss of your wealth.
To wear them: Evil influences are with you.
To break one: Somebody will betray you.

Ears

To see big ones: There is false gossip about you.
To clean your ears: Your marriage brings you many benefits.
To be blocked: You will be confronted with falsehoods.
To see many of them: Disturbances in your environment.

Earthquake

Be careful at pedestrian crossings.

Earthworms

To see a few: You acquire a new circle of acquaintances.
To buy them as bait for fishing: Do not slack off just because you are feeling bored with your routine.

Earwig

Someone will try to delude you.

Easel

To stand in front of it and draw: A certain amount of secrecy where business is concerned would be valuable.

Easter

Trust in God and your mental anguish will disappear.

Easter eggs	To eat them: A big profit in the near future.
Easter Sunday	To have a party: You have the opportunity to break into high society.
Easy chair	To see or sit in one: Follow through on a hunch and realize that first impressions are most apt to be correct.
Eavesdropper	To be one: You will experience disgrace.
Echo	To hear one: You will have pleasant visitors. To shout one: Don't talk too much. It could be harmful for you. Not to hear one: A friend needs your help.
Eclipse of the moon	To see one: You should take steps towards obtaining a greater degree of security.
Edelweiss	To see one: A sense of obligation may pull you in several directions at once.
Editor's office	Have confidence in yourself.
Eggs	To eat them: Your interest in art will bring you pleasure and profit. To see them: Beauty plays an important role in romance. To break them: Do not be surprised if others sometimes mistake your natural reserve for shyness.
Eggshells	To see them: You are to blame if something unpleasant should happen to you.
Eggwhite	To whisk it: Quick and casual friendships do not come easily to you.
Elbows	Marital affairs that have been flagging can be revitalized.
Elderbush	To see it in bloom: A very special and lucky love-life. To pick elderberries: You will recover from an old problem.
Election	Your best course of action would be to back away.
Electricity	To get a shock: Don't blame your wife; she doesn't deserve it.
Electric light	You receive a very important letter that you have been waiting for.

Elephant	To see one: A very small barrier will disrupt your daily routine.
Elevator	To be in one: In romance, take care to avoid indiscretion.
Embroidery	To do it yourself: Avoid extravagance. Respect the work of others.
Emerald	To dream about one: Means bad luck.
Emigrant	To see them on a boat: Friends or relatives will be helpful and will do all that they can to make you feel at home.
Employee	To see one of yours: Take care of future expenses.
Emporer	To see him: Influential people can disappoint you.
Empress	To see her: You will have need of something.
Encore	To call for an encore: A reunion with friends is in the near future.
Encyclopedia	To look something up: A stubborn associate is advocating a path that would be foolishly extravagant.
Enemies	To defeat them: Affliction overcomes you.
Engaged	To be: It is unwise to be selfish.
Engine	To see one: Professional advice may prove to be very helpful. To see a disabled one: Misery in your family. To repair one: Improve your business and move to another location.
Enter	Carry on as you are.
Entrance	To a house: See what you can do to add value and beauty to your surroundings. To a church: You will regain your dignity.
Epilepsy	You are in a good position to win in a lottery or in gambling.
Epitaph	To see or read one: A vacation would be invaluable to your health.
Equilibrium	To hold your balance: Career matters should take preference over personal issues.

Ermine	To see one in a cage: Take care to avoid hasty actions.
Escape	If you dream about an escape: It means that a dangerous situation prevails.
Essence	To use it: Avoid quarrels and misunderstandings.
Eskimos	To be with them: You will have reason to complain about unfaithfulness.
Estate	To live in one: Don't be so lavish. To purchase one: Some interesting ideas could arise from discussions with your family about ways to increase the value of your home. To see one: You must not allow feelings of depression to get to you.
Eunuch	To see one: In case of a lawsuit, hire a well-known lawyer.
Europe	To see or travel through: A gain of money plus a good business connection is a possibility if you travel.
Evening bell	If you hear the ring in your dream: You can expect to be freed from heartache or to free loved ones from sadness or trouble. If you ring the bell: Sickness will strike you.
Evening leisure	It is important to pay attention to home improvement.
Evening star	To see its appearance: This usually promises complete recovery from an illness. For a person in love: Truthfulness of your partner. If the star is dull and covered with clouds: A beloved person is in danger.
Examine	To do: You are unable to hide your secret fears.
Examinations	To write one: Don't criticize your best friend; it may be misinterpreted.
Excavation	To dig up a treasure: Be sure that you pay attention to all safety regulations when at work.
Exchange	Don't borrow any money. If you do, be sure that you are able to pay it back on time.
Excitement	You will be confronted with the truth and that will put you in an awkward position.

Excoriate	An animal: A dishonorable mutation is in progress.
Excrement	To step in: It may be a good idea to invest in precious metals. To collect it: Although your efforts may not be quickly rewarded, someday you may be a wealthy person.
Excuse	To use an excuse in your dream: Your family will not make any special demands upon you.
Executed	To be: Be more concerned about your health. To see someone who will be executed: There is a danger of accidents if you allow your mind to wander while on the job. To execute someone: You will be dishonored by your peers.
Executioner	To see him in action: Bereavement due to death of domestic animals. To talk to him: Forfeit your honorable reputation. If he touches your body: You will soon commit a crime.
Exercise	You will be promoted very soon.
Exile	Your situation will change overnight.
Expel	You may receive a citation.
Expenses	To have them: In order that your interests are protected, make sure that all agreements are in writing.
Experiment	To do one: You have good ideas, but you never have the courage to put them into motion.
Exploration	To make one: Most of your life will be satisfying and pleasurable.
Explosion	To witness one: Disappointed hopes.
Express letter	To get one: You could experience a disappointment in the morning, but the afternoon brings a wonderful recovery.
Express train	To ride in one: Be more vigorous. To see one leaving the station: Your desire will not be fulfilled.
Extinguish	A fire: Your future will be a happy one.

Eye glasses

To wear them: Beware of temptation.
To see people wearing glasses: Beware of wicked persons who will try to infiltrate your relationships.
To lose them: People will be nosey and inquisitive, but you should not let them in on your plans.
To see glasses laying around: Do not paint too black a picture of your family, home and domestic difficulties.
To wear colored glasses: Be careful with your face and your eyes.

Eyes

To see blue ones: What you have determined will steer you in the right direction.
To see brown ones: A visit to your doctor should help clear up any minor ailment that has been troubling you.
To see crossed eyes: All kinds of losses may occur.
To see blinded eyes: A personal plan may have to be altered.
To see closed eyes: Someone is in love with you, but you don't yet realize it.
To see eyebrows: What sounds like an excellent idea for making some fast money will probably not pan out.

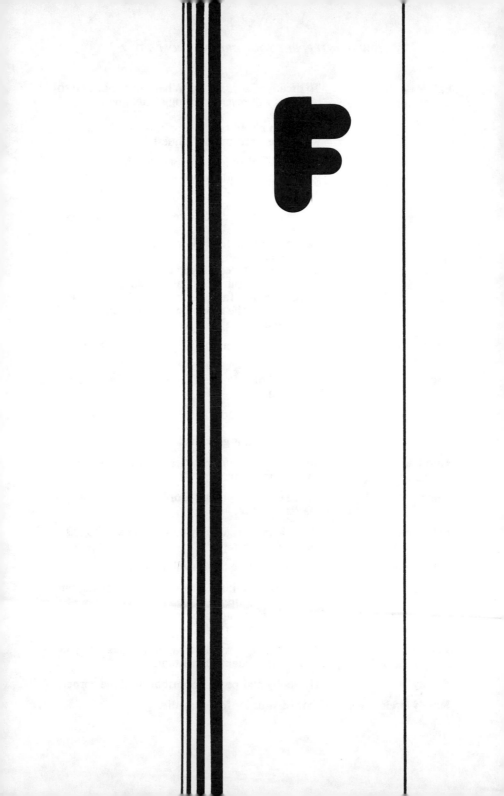

F

Fabric	To dream of soft fabric: What once appeared to be a loss will revert to being something favorable. To dream about rough fabric: A family member will make a reasonable request.
Face	To see your face in a mirror: Health and a long life. To see a pretty face: You will triumph over an opponent. To see an ugly face: You regret your wrong doings. To see a strange face: Secret transactions are favorable. To see a pale face: All you can do is to try and cut down on your personal spending. To see a baby's face: An idea that you were hoping to get off the ground can now be implemented.
Factory	To be in one: You don't have to worry about your business.
Fair	To attend one: Success will follow minor disappointments.
Fairy	Parents should do what they can to get closer to their children. This also means good luck.
Fairytale	To hear one: Your activities and performances will be successful.
Falcon	To see one in captivity: Don't be frivolous in matters of love.
Fall asleep	You will be intrigued by an individual who has an aura of mystery.
Fall down	Somebody close to you will become ill.
Falling	To see leaves falling: Prospect of money-making in the near future. To see fruit falling from trees: Uncertain fortunes and pleasures.
Fame	To have it: You would have more success if you kept your thoughts consistent.
Family	Harmony and peace are just around the corner.
Family circle	One of your kinfolk may die.

Fan

To see an old one: A family member has to go out of town on a business trip.
To see one in motion: Take the opportunity to get a clear picture of your financial situation.

Fanfare

To hear one: Inflation and war.

Fancy-dress ball

To see one: Hypocrites surround you.

Farewell

A farewell from a visitor: Your energy is not strong enough for you to proceed with your project.
A farewell from a lover is a constant reminder of faithfulness.
A goodbye from a friend is an indication of previous happiness between the two of you.

Farm

To live on one: Good luck in all of your undertakings.

Farmer

To see him working: Your future will be blessed. You will attain success through struggles and patience.
To see a young farmer or his wife: You will get a complicated job which will be satisfactory and permanent.
To see a young farmer's girl: You will marry an ambitious person.
To do business with a farmer: An unexpected inheritance.

Farm hand

To see one working with animals: You will have to put a great deal more effort into your regular job.
To see him quarrelling: Any speculation should be avoided.

Farmhouse

To see an old, rundown farmhouse: You are living in a state of poverty, but you are satisfied with your surroundings and have no great desire to alter your position.

Farmyard

To be in one: You will make good progress.

Fashion magazine

You will be criticized.

Fashion shop

Your girl-friend will not invite you to her wedding.

Fast

Time of fasting: Through your appearance you give the impression of dignity and honor.

Fat person   To see one: Try to stick to a nutritious diet.

Father   To be one: Now you are becoming self-reliant, independent, and are expressing many of your positive qualities.

Father-in-law   To dream about him means: You will be rewarded by success.

Favor   To refuse someone a favor: It may bring your hostility to a peak.

Fear   To have: Stand up for your principles.
It can also mean: Disappointment and misfortune in love.
To experience fear: An insult may be expected.

Feast   To witness one: Your employer will grant your request.

Feathers   To see them: Your wishes come true.

Fee   To pay a fee: You will experience a financial loss.

Feed   To feed your pet: It is time to move on and be rid of burdens which were not rightly yours in the first place.
To feed wild animals: Members of the opposite sex find you attractive.

Feeding trough   To see an empty one: Grief and distress.
To see a full one: Don't be stubborn and just decide to go ahead with your plans without considering the possible consequences of your actions.

Feet   To see someone's: Watch your enemies.
To break your own: Postpone your marriage.
To see broken ones: Don't allow greedy relatives to drain your reserves.
To wash your feet: You may be able to clear up health problems.
To see dirty feet: You had better get rid of a friend who is a bad influence on you.

Felt slipper   To see or wear them: You have ample opportunity to discuss important issues with your family.

Fence   To see one: Look closely at people who will visit you.

To step over one: You should feel more energetic about starting your new project.
To see an old one: Your romance will be trouble free.

Fern   You are immodest and a slave to your passions.

Ferry   To be on one: You have a hard time convincing your family that you must be allowed to do your own thing.

Festivity   To attend a festive event: It is about time to find an outlet for the artistic side of your nature.

Festive procession   Happiness and pleasure within your family.

Fetch   Some peculiar demands are made on you.

Fetter   Honesty always pays.

Feuilleton   To read: Your own negligence causes you to suffer a financial loss.

Fever   To have one: You will be happy without being wealthy.

Fiancée   To talk to her: Time is on your side.

Fiddle   To play one: You will receive a wedding invitation.

Fiddlestick   To see one: Your present unpleasant situation will soon change.

Field   To cultivate one: Your new position enables you to be more independent.
To see a devastated one: Distress and misery is the future of your homeland.
To walk in a field: You may lose money or goods and must be careful in speculations.

Field of corn   To see one: You will get some cooperation from colleagues.

Field of grain   To harvest one: Good times are coming.

Field of rape   The time is right to get involved in negotiations and contracts.

Fight   To see one: You may have to face danger.
To get involved in one: Misfortune in your business or projects.

Figs   To buy or eat them: Success in love.

Filberts   To pick them: Take good care of your health.
To eat them: You will overcome unpleasant things.

Finch   To see one: Don't count your chickens before they are hatched.

Fingers   To see beautiful ones: You are applauded for your creative activities.
To see them covered with blood: Your plans will succeed if they are handled intelligently.

Fir   To see one: You perceive trend and profit as a result of your undertakings.
To cut one: A pleasing surprise will be sprung upon you.

Fir needles   To see them: Your romance is active.

Fire   To see a fire with bright flames: Lots of happiness and good are forthcoming.
To see a fire with dark smoke: You may feel sadness and disappointment in the near future.
To be at the scene of a fire: Don't put all of your initiative into one project - keep other options open.
To see a fire in a stove: Your children are not under the best supervision.
To extinguish a fire: You will get yourself into financial trouble.
To see a house on fire: You are bad-tempered -try to change it.

Fireplace   With fire: Look into tax and insurance matters.
Without fire: Domestic differences will arise, probably over money.
To sit in front of it: You are fortunate, government officials are accommodating.

Fireworks   To see them: One who aided in the past will reappear.

Firmament   With many stars: A very big inheritance in the near future.

Fish   To eat fish: Luck in lottery and gambling.
To catch fish: Disorder within the family.
To buy fish: Be cautious, people are not always honest.
To see a small fish: Disputes with your spouse.

To see one swimming: Your love will not be returned.
To see many of them: You do not have many good friends.
To receive one as a gift: Someone is trying to persuade you.

Fish bones   To see them on your plate: You are fighting disagreeableness.

Fishermen   To see them fishing: You will be the winner.

Fishing-net   To work with one: An enormous profit is in sight.

Fish market   To be in one: A superior, however sincere, could be misinformed.

Fishing-tackle   To be occupied with: Warnings of fraud and cunning artifice.

Fist   To see your own fist: If you get into a dispute, it will be your own fault.

Flag   To carry one: You will be admired by many people.

Flail   To dream about it: You will marry a hot-tempered person.

Flame   To see one: The problems of relatives can be handled satisfactorily.
To extinguish it: More time should be given to planning correspondence.

Flat-iron   To buy one: There is a strong possibility of deception and fraud.
To repair a broken one: Obscure information may still be coming to light, but you should not be too optimistic about it.

Flattery   You are on the right track if you follow your inner voice.

Fleas   To see them: Your greediness will give you a hard time.
To get stung by them: You will hear unpleasant matters.
To see them jump: Your cleverness will bring you over a hump.

Flies   To try to catch them: You learn a secret.

To have them in a room: Watch that temper of yours.

To see one in a drink: Try to stop one of your bad habits.

Flirtation

With a girl: Maintain a sense of humor about yourself.

With a man: A letter or a phone call will bring you good news.

Float

To see one on a shore: You must be careful not to overlook minor details.

To see one float down a river: You will be surrounded by loneliness.

Flood

To dream about a flood means: Your debtors won't give you any peace.

Floor

To see a dirty floor: Troubles and food problems within your family.

To clean a parquet floor: You may have the opportunity to sort out problems that have been plaguing your personal life.

Flour

To sift it: You may become wealthy in the near future.

Flowers

To see them blooming: You will push your luck away.

To pick flowers: A strong relationship that is formed now has a better chance of lasting.

To dream about a flower shop means: Sadness will pass quickly.

To see a flower basket: A jealous admirer will spread nasty gossip about you.

To buy a flowerpot: Means that you are disappointed in your actions and hopes.

To plant flowers in a pot: A mistake could ruin your reputation.

Flute

To hear someone playing the flute: You will be able to make plans for the future quite successfully.

To play the flute yourself: You make a significant breakthrough.

Flutter

To see a bird: You will reach your goal, but you must be patient.

Fly

To fly in an airplane: Your generosity will bring good results and good friends.

Foam

To touch it: Love is not always true.
To see foam-covered water: Easy come, easy go.
To see the foam of soap: To live and work in a foreign country will bring success and wealth.

Fog

To see the mist come in: Don't let someone persuade you.
To see heavy fog: Sometimes it is very hard to understand your own behavior.
To drive through fog: Loved ones do care, and you will become more aware of it.
To see fog rising from the ground: Your future is stable.

Fog-horn

To hear one: If your goal is to be more successful, your dreams will come true.

Font

To see one: You will receive help from somebody you never expected it from.

Food

Trouble through your own behavior.

Fool

To see or to talk to him: Your position is stronger than it appears on the surface.
To be one: People tease you.

Fool's cap

To see one: You will fall in love very soon.
To wear one: You will make a fool of yourself.

Football

Improve your activities in sports or gymnastics. It will be good for your health and your mind.

Footstool

To see one: The coming years will be easy and delightful.,
To stand on one: You will find it valuable to do a certain amount of experimenting.

Forest

To walk through a forest: You will feel sorry for a good friend.

Forester

To see one at work: Do not gamble with money that you can't afford to lose.

Forest fire

To see one: You are very knowledgeable in your job or profession.

Forget-me-not

To see some: Make peace with your spouse.
To give them away: You can trust your spouse.

Forgive

Somebody: Lady luck is on your side.

Fork

To drop a fork: Some misfortune is following you.

	To eat with one: There may be some interruptions due to a health problem of a loved one.
Fortress	To force things is not always right.
Fortune teller	To be one: Dreams are nearer to becoming a reality than you think. If you listen to one: Opportunities multiply.
Foundling	Unfaithfulness in your marriage will make you very unhappy.
Fountain	To see one: You will discover a secret.
Fox	To hunt one: You will discover that a friend of yours is a double-dealer.
Fracture	Somewhere in your body: With your luck you will have a prosperous future.
Fragments of glass	To see them: Avoid extravagance.
Frail	To be: You are worried about your future.
Frame	To frame a picture: Keep an eye on your business partner. He may not be working in your favor.
Freeze to death	To dream about it means: What had once been far away is now within your reach.
Freezer	To fill up your freezer: The extra cash that you should be getting must not be spent impulsively.
French horn	To hear one in your dream: A member of the opposite sex does care and you will gradually become aware of it.
Friend	To see one: Inconveniences. To talk to one: Don't ignore people who are helpful to you.
Fretwork	To do: With your talent, you should try to enter an art school.
Frogs	To watch them jump: Setbacks are transformed into victories. To hear them croak: Obey all safety rules to avoid mishaps. To see them in the water: You are homesick. To see a green one: A pay raise is possible. To kill them: Your behavior is not the best; you will harm yourself. To eat frog-legs: You have a protector.

Frost
To see it on the grass: Unpleasant experiences with business partners.
To feel it: Hypocritic people look for your friendship.

Fruits
To harvest them: Your position is stronger than originally anticipated.
To buy them: Don't let yourself be fooled.
To see them displayed: You are very smart, and this is why you will reach your goal.
To see them on a tree: Very good expectations.
To eat sweet fruits: You will meet very pleasant people.
To preserve them: Move away from your present home. You have enemies there.
To give them away: Profit is on the way.

Fruit market
To be in one: Success in your enterprises.

Fruit tree
In blossom: Don't worry, other people are no better than you are.

Fruit wine
To drink it: Your yearning will soon be fulfilled.

Frying
To see something: Through hard work you will reach your goal.

Frying-pan
To use one over a fire: Good outlook for better times.
To see a broken one: Unpleasant visitors will arrive.

Full score
To write one: You will be honored.

Funeral
To see yourself being buried: For married people, your family grows.
For single people: Marriage soon.
With a relative's corpse: Marriage as wished.
To watch a funeral procession: Your good manners will one day help you get a very well-paid and distinguished position.
To attend a funeral procession: Luck and enjoyment.

Funeral home
To dream about one: Someone whom you admire very much will die.

Funeral march
To play one: Romance should work out well if you make the first move.

Funnel
To see one: Take good care of the things which are most important to you.

Funny   To be: It is an omen that a temporary sickness will soon end.
To see somebody else: Don't hide anything from your partners.

Furnace   To see one: Be careful who you trust; do not let too many people in on your future plans.
To get burned by one: Speculation could be disastrous; you must avoid any gambling.

Furniture   To buy it: There is a limit to everything.
To polish it: This indicates degradation and a loss of inheritance.

Furs   To dream about furs means: Sickness and anxiety.

Fury   To dream about it means: Don't be revengeful.

Gale

To be caught in one: You must free yourself from trouble.

Gallery

To see an art gallery: You will receive important news.
If you see many people in one: Give serious thought to matters connected with the future.

Galley

To see one: Your surroundings will be jeopardized.

Gallop

To be galloping: You will surely overcome obstacles.

Gallows

To see one: Time will be unstable and you should be aware of false friends.

Gambling

In a casino: Keep spending on entertainment to a minimum.

Games

You play it on a board: Uncertain success in business.

Gangster

To see: Don't delay - ask your best friend for help.

Garbage

To see it: You are on the way to success.
To walk in: It is an especially good time for making decisions.

Garden

If you dream of a garden: It is a very good omen which means luck and success in all of your actions.

Garden tools

You will have a worry-free future.

Garland

To carry: You may lose some valuables.
A green one: Fulfillment of your wishes.
With roses: Respect your parents.
To see one on a door: Your next holiday will be full of nice surprises.

Garlic

To smell it in a dream: Nuisances coming up.
To eat: Quarrels with your brother or sister.

Garrison

To be associated with: You will start up a business and your wish for a new home will come true.

Garter

To see one: You will have some trouble with your spouse.
To find one: Disaster will pursue you.

Gas	To cook on: Very soon your hopes will become reality. To see gaslight: There are many jobs that you can cope with from within the comfort and security of your own four walls.
Gasoline	Arguments are likely to break out at home.
Gate	To see: A very happy marriage will soon happen.
Gears	To see at work: Do whatever you can by yourself; don't ask for help.
Gelatine	To dream about means: Don't depend on your friends.
Gem	Do plenty of reading. Gain through written words.
General	To see or be one: Don't do anything voluntarily right now. It could cause you trouble.
Gentleman	To appear as one: You will hear an insult.
Genuflexion	Bending of the knee as if worshipping: You will lose your privileges.
Ghost	To see a ghost in a dream: You have to resist a temptation in the near future.
Giant	To see one: Exotic overseas travel.
Gift	To receive one: You will travel more during your lifetime than the average person does. To give one to somebody: It is hard for you to find a true love.
Giggle	To hear one: Your clumsy behavior is self-mocking.
Gin	To drink it: Adhere to basic principles. Finish rather than initiate projects.
Gingerbread	To make or eat it: A healthy and happy outlook on life.
Giraffe	To see one in a zoo: Earlier losses will be recovered.
Girl	To see one: Romance offers opportunity for a more permanent relationship.

To see one play: Romance may contain misunderstandings.
To see one in prayer: Don't lose your confidence.

Giving

To give somebody something in a dream: Don't embarrass people.

Glass

To see a pane of glass: If you are involved in a lawsuit, it will turn out in your favor. It also means a bright future.
To see broken glass: Sickness within your family.
To cut a glass by yourself: Marriage within the next year.
To see a full glass: You have pleasant opportunities.
To see an empty glass: You will feel unwelcome on your next visit.
To see a lot of glasses: An invitation to a happy occasion.

Glider

To see one in the air: Treasure hunting will turn out successful for you.

Globe

To see one: You may have to postpone your next trip.

Gloves

To put gloves on: Be careful with what you say.
To take gloves off: Trouble and arguments.
To buy gloves and try them on: An omen of a long journey.

Glow-worm

To see one: You are always too frank.

Glue

To buy or work with it: Speak up - you don't agree with everything all the time.

Go astray

You are not able to complete your proposal because you cannot keep silent.

Goat

To see one: You are often in a bad mood - try to change it.
To see a black one: Now is time to apply finishing touches.

Goblet

To see one: You will meet somebody who you have not seen for a long time.
To buy one: Luck and comfort.
To drink out of one: You can expect a very good time.

	To see it fall or break: Trouble and unexpected misfortune.
Godfather	To see or become one: Unexpected honor lies ahead of you.
Goiter	To see one on someone: Do not act on information passed on to you by another person. To have one yourself: A good idea will bring you relief.
Gold	To see or have: Continuous success in present and future undertakings. To wear: Your attitude is unreliable. To find: Luck and inheritance. To lose or pay with gold: A breakup between friends and problems with your business. To receive a gold barren: False impressions, trouble and sickness. To dig for gold: Your happiness is not where you expect it, but it will surprisingly surface.
Goldfish	Your happiness will leave you.
Gold mine	To find one: Your winnings are a sure thing.
Gold paper	To see or have: You will find it easier to see eye to eye with relatives with whom you have not been getting along recently.
Golf	To be playing: Soon you will get an answer for your question. To see others play: Do not deal with problems that can easily be left until the work week ahead.
Goose	To see one: Gossip about you. To buy one: You will become someone's fool. To see a roasted goose: The health of your loved ones should be another source of worry for you. To slaughter one: Inheritance can be expected. To see them flying: A long journey ahead.
Gooseberries	To eat them: You will learn where you stand in connection with a special person.
Gospel	To read: Spend a quiet evening with one who really cares for you.
Gossip	To hear: You will receive a wedding invitation. To be interested in gossip: The result of your recent business trip will turn out satisfactorily.

Gout
To have in a dream: Most people think you are easy to influence; that's why you have to fight so often.

Government
If you have something to do with the government in a dream: You will soon be reconciled with your acquaintances.

Grain
To sow: Employed people may obtain favors from their superiors.
To harvest: Teamwork will bring you excellent results.
To see: You may find that you need to pay more attention to your health.

Grammar
To study: Through hard work you achieve family happiness.

Grammar school
To be at one: Through knowledge you will attain authority.
To be a school boy or girl at one in a dream: You will have talented children.

Gramophone
To play one: Discord and bad luck at home.

Grandfather
To see or speak to him: Comfort and happiness. Also, don't hesitate to show your employer what you really can do.

Grandmother
To see or speak to her: You will lead a good undertaking to completion.

Grapes
To see them: Your health is steady.
To eat them: Family differences will not be settled.
To see them unripened: You will reach your goal.
To plant them: You will promote your luck.
To harvest them: Happiness at home.

Grass
To walk on it: You will attend a funeral.
To see it very green: A lost friend will reappear.
To see it dried up: Your health is unstable.
To cut it: You have a chance to win something.
To pick it: It may be a sign of a dangerous sickness.
To eat it: A case of death.

Grasshoppers
To see them: You may have some problems to cope with, either in the personal or in the public area.
To hear them: You will hear some terrible news.

To kill them: You will cause damage to your neighbors.

Grating

To see one: You must free yourself from egotistic thoughts.

Grave

To see one: Be discreet - don't talk about secrets friends have entrusted to you.
To dig one: Be more careful with your language, otherwise you will be in big trouble.
To see it being closed in: Your health will decline if you don't change your mode of living.
To see one with flowers on top: If you feel sorry about yourself all the time, your life will be miserable.

Grave digger

To see one at work: Uncomfortable moments, but the end result will be new peace of mind.

Gravel

To see or work with: A good omen of luck, good harvesting and an inheritance.

Graveyard

See "cemetery".

Greade

To see: One day you will become wealthy.

Great dane

To see one: Always go a straight way.
To get bitten by one: Delegate some of your work before you put yourself into a dangerous corner.

Greek

To see or speak to one: You are advancing in your accomplishment.

Green

To see a green garment: Means good fortune.
To see green color: Prosperous hopes and wishes come true.

Greenhouse

To see or be in one: To start now is better than never. If you don't plant, you cannot expect harvest.

Greyhound

Make the decision now or you will lose the success.

Grief

To be in grief in a dream: If you work on it, your wishes will come true.
To see somebody be in grief: Take necessary steps to protect yourself from loss.

Grind

You welcome guests in your home.

Grindstone

You are given increased responsibility.

Grocer   To see or speak to one: Do not invest capital without weighing all the pros and cons first.

Grow   To see something grow in your dream: Do some personal detective work in order to bring light to some family secrets you always wanted to know.

Ground   Covered with moss: You will marry into money. Stony and rough: You struggle without success.

Groundplan   To make or see one: You will receive some welcome news about an investment.

Guard   You see one or more guards: A romance will come to an end.

Guest   To have one: Influential people will like your style.
To be a guest: Professional advice will be important if you are dealing with insurance or real estate matters.

Guinea fowl   To see one: Success.

Guinea pig   To see one: Avoid a long journey if you possibly can.

Guitar   To play one: Pleasant times ahead.

Gulf   To see one: Your plan to travel to other cities is likely to turn out to be far too expensive and a complete waste of time.

Guns   To see or hear them: You are innocent in one of your friend's misfortunes.
Hunting trip with a gun: Unfaithfulness.
To shoot a gun: Lies, jealousy and fraud.
To load a gun: Your undertakings will be fruitless.
To see a beautiful gun: You will fall in love.

Gunboat   To see a gunboat in a dream: A change will bring you no pleasure.

Gunner   Losses can be serious and may be quite sudden.

Gunpowder   To see: Be aware of a crime which may occur near to your home.

Gutter   To see one: The next days could be the calm before the storm.

Gutterpipe   To see one on a house: You will find a good partner.

Gypsum   If you see gypsum or work with it: This is a very good sign of friendship and pleasure and foretells of your wealthiness.

Gypsy   To see or speak to one: You are in a position to make a mistake.

Hail

To see it: You have an expensive friendship which will end in ingratitude.
To be in a hailstorm: Your wishes and hopes will not be realized because of unkindness, trouble, or treason.

Hair

To see it: This means good fortune.
To see very long hair: This signifies healthiness and power.
To cut your own hair: Be aware of a possible loss.
To see hair on your hands: Unexpected money.
To lose hair: Warns of a harmless, but long and drawn-out illness.
To see or have blond hair: A love affair brings you confusion.
To see or have dark hair: You will attain an honored and respected position.

Hairdresser

To see one at work: You will make a great impact on the world and will gain wider recognition.
To be one: You will be lucky in all of your business affairs.

Hall

To see or dance in a big hall: Money may show a tendency to slip right through your fingers.

Hallelujah

To sing it: Your success will be enormous.

Halter

To put one on a horse: Don't neglect your business; most of the people involved think you are too lavish.

Ham

If you eat ham in your dream: A chance to participate in a profitable enterprise presents itself.

Hammer

To work with one: Misery is forthcoming.
To see someone work with one: A long-awaited affirmative answer will come from a friend.

Hamster

To see one: Your old age will be free of worries.

Hand

To see your hands: Be careful - somebody would like to start a quarrel.
To see big hands: Discord with your spouse.
To see very clean hands: You have true friends.
To see dirty hands: Control your debauchery.
To give somebody a handshake: You will need the help of a stranger. It can also mean that you will help another in need.

Hand bell
To hear one: Right now is the time to seek a loan, as bankers will be easier to influence.

Handcuffs
To see them on yourself: No luck in sight.
To see them on somebody else: Be aware of the possibility of an accident.

Hand gun
To hear one fire: Success will come easily, but you must continue to work very hard.
One fires in your hand: Use and depend upon your own judgment in a difficult situation.

Handkerchief
To see or use one: Your dependents may be taken for granted too often.
A silk one: Annoyance within the family.
To use a very white one: Don't complain; you should be very happy.

Harbor
To see or to arrive at a harbor: Good luck and happiness will follow a worrisome and stressful time.

Harem
To be in one: You are living a life of pleasure.

Harmonica
To hear one being played: You will hold a festive party.

Harlot
To be in the company of a harlot: Your conscience indicates that there is another way to release yourself from your recent troubles. Don't be violent.

Harp
If you play one: You may take an exploratory trip.
To see a girl playing one: You don't seem to care much about your health. You should take steps to remedy this.

Harvest
To see: The clouds of confusion will be erased and you will have a more realistic view.
To carry in: Financial gain is the result of a good business or stock investment.

Harvester
At work: Your reputation may be tarnished.
In the shade: Don't be afraid; everything will be alright.
To talk to one: At the last minute you will reach your goal.

Haste
To have: If you strike a better balance between work and play, your family life will be more rewarding.

To have haste and be immobile: You will have a dispute with somebody.

Hat

To wear one: Your impulsive decision will be a lucky one.
To see or wear one with feathers: Foretells of honor.
To lose a hat: Loss of respect.

Hat box

For a healthy person: You will receive a gift.
For an ill person: A prolonged recovery from your illness.

Hatchet

To see one or to work with one: Be aware of a dangerous venture, one in which you have little or no control over.
To sharpen a hatchet: Many quarrels and much anger.

Hawk

To see one: Don't allow others to influence your spending habits.

Hay

To see pretty hay: The coming days will definitely be good for business.
To smell it: This means good health.
To see a hay wagon: You should be feeling much happier about the future.

Hayloft

Filled with hay: Growing wealth and prosperity.
To see an empty one: This reminds you not to be so lazy.

Hazelnut

To pick or to try to find them: You will get into arguments with your neighbors.
To eat them: You may lose some teeth.
To see a hazel bush: Your partner will share some good news about a family matter.

Head

To see your own: Time doesn't permit the necessary force to sustain a new beginning.
To see a bare one: Everybody admires you.
To wash your own: The coming weeks will free you from unpleasantness.

Headache

To have one: You will be involved in a lawsuit.

Health resort

To be at one: Someone you feel is on your side may let you down.

Hearing

To lose your: You will become depressed and if you are not careful, poor, too.

Hearse   To see one in a dream: You will receive an unfavorable message.

Heart   To see an artificial one made of some material or sweets: You should never have to worry about making a living, as you are a person with artistic skills.
To have a fast heartbeat or pains: This is rarely a dream version. Most likely, these are real feelings of pain produced within your body.

Heat   To feel heat in a dream: Don't ignore health problems. You should give adequate attention to minor ailments.

Heaven's gate   To stay at: A happy message will soon reach you.

Heaven's ladder To see one: If you are expecting favors from other people, you will have problems.

Hedge   To see one: If you are single, you will soon be married.
For others: You will soon complain about your workload.

Hedgehog   To see one: All assaults against you will be unsuccessful.

Hell   To see it: Risky ventures, however, attractive they may appear, must be avoided.
To be in: You will fall into the hands of mean and unscrupulous persons.
To be freed from: You will find help and understanding.

Helmet   To wear one: Give a special treat to the person you hold dearest.

Hemp   To see or work with it: You will be hindered in all of your undertakings.
To sow hemp: You will have many struggles and lots of hard work, without much profit to show for it.

Hen   To see one lay eggs: A happy occasion ahead.
To see one with chicks: Foretells of happiness and good luck.
To see one without a tail: You will lose your respect.

Herald   To dream about one: You will receive important news.

Herbs   To eat them: You hold the advantage in everything you do.
To pick them: This is a good time for those of you applying for jobs.

Herd   To see one in a field: Unexpected gain is the end result of a joint venture.
To see one eating: Your natural reserve with money will serve to protect you in the coming weeks.
To find yourself in the middle of one: You are not thinking before you act.

Hermit   To see or to be one: Postpone travel arrangements for a couple of days.
If you see a friend as a hermit: Have more confidence in yourself.

Heron   To see one: Although you are very attractive to the opposite sex, you must not blame others for any disadvantage you may have.

Herring   To eat one: If you are considering borrowing some money, carefully think twice about whether you really need it.

Hide   Yourself: You are creative, at times self-centered, sensual, independent, stubborn, original, inventive, and attractive to members of the opposite sex.
If you play hide-and-seek in a dream: You are responsible for allowing yourself to fall from an advanced position.

Hide   To tan the hide of animals: You will sustain a loss.

High mass To be present at one: There will soon be a lot of happiness.

High school To be in one: You are in bad company; look for new friends.

High tide To see it: Ill-begotten gain never thrives.

Highway   To drive on one: You will have a pleasant trip. This also signifies good business affairs.
To walk on one: It would be wise if you would share fewer secrets.

Hike   To take one: Your health can be improved if you watch your diet and get yourself into better shape by exercising.

Hills To climb: Be prepared to shoulder heavier responsibilities.

Hinny (mule) To ride on one: An enemy will cheat you.

Hoar frost On a field: A hope will be destroyed.
On a meadow: Be aware of bad luck.
On the roof: Your dignity is only one facet of your behavior.
In the cellar: Don't deviate from the truth. Honesty always pays.

Hoary To be: This means that you will have a long line of descendants.

Hoarseness To have: You will come out ahead and win.

Hole If you see a hole in the wall: Foretells of a lawsuit.
To see one in a dress or in a suit: Do not go along with any proposed gambling schemes.
To drill one: Your effort is fruitless.

Holster To see one: You will take a journey.

Holy To see holy people: Good things will happen.
To worship a holy person: You are not fully committed to your religion.

Holy communion Being part of: An old friendship will be in jeopardy unless you change your attitudes.

Holiday To dream of one: Your intention to break up a friendship will end in disappointment.

Homeland To see your homeland in a dream: Pleasant times and happy hours are ahead of you.

Honey To buy it: Winning and success in business.
To eat it: Undesirability and melancholy are in the future.

Honorarium To receive one: A happy occasion arrives unexpectedly.

Hop To see a hop field: You will have a bitter experience.
To grow hops. For those of you in a business partnership, this is a very prosperous time.

Horn   To hear one: Your love is not returned.

Hornet   To see one: Be aware of the possibility of fire.
                            To be stung by one: You will suffer because of
                            misunderstandings.

Hornet's nest   If you see one: Everything on this earth is
                            perishable. Think about it.

Horses   To see them: It is important that you are extra
                            careful and do not take any risks.
                            To see a white one: You will go into mourning.
                            To see a wounded one: Misery and poverty.
                            To see a dead one: Sad news comes from far
                            away.
                            If you see one overturned: Your enemies will be
                            the victors.
                            To see a skinny one: Something will impede your
                            progress.
                            To drive them to pasture: Somebody in a high
                            position will promote you.
                            To see a horse race: You will lose a good friend.
                            To ride on a horse: Don't take so many risks.

Horseshoe   To see or find one: Luck in business or other
                            plans.
                            If you mount a horseshoe: Honor and dignity.
                            To see someone mount a horseshoe: A big sur-
                            prise and good luck are in store for you.

Hospital   To see one: A very unpleasant situation will soon
                            come to an end.
                            To be in one: One who ignored you in the past
                            admits his error.

Host   To be one: Your lifestyle allows you to feel com-
                            fortable and peaceful with yourself.

Hostel   To see a lodge or to live in one: You are becom-
                            ing poor.

Hotel   To see or to be in one: You will go through a lot
                            of money.

Hotwater bottle   Be sure and lock your doors to protect your
                            valuables.

House   To build one: A difficult situation will most like-
                            ly resolve itself.
                            To buy one: This will be a fortunate period for
                            you.

To sell one: Seek professional legal advice before you become involved in a matter which could take you before a court.
This also signifies losses.
To tear one down: Authoritative figures will be scrutinizing your actions.
To see one fall down: Postpone any business transactions until such time that you are more optimistic and better able to cope.
To see an old one in need of repair: Sickness and worries.

Household utensils

To clean and organize them: Work of any kind is likely to be profitable.
To see them in your dream: You will have the willpower to stick to any diet that you decide to start or to cut down on smoking or drinking.

Housemaster

To be one: Your wellbeing will improve.
To see one: You won't get your fair share.

House porter

To see or to be one: Don't make any financial commitments right now.

Houseshoe

To walk in: An overall improvement is indicated.

Housewife

To see yourself as one: Your parent or spouse will try to help you in any way they can.

Howling

To hear: Be cautious when using any tools or machinery.

Hug

Somebody: Use tact and charm to achieve your goals.

Humble

To feel submissive: This is always an omen that happiness and good times are ahead.
For people in love: Happy endings.

Humpback

To see one: Good results in every aspect.
To see yourself with a hump: Large winnings.
To bend down: Be aware of some loss. Someone may be trying to tarnish your reputation.

Hunger

To be hungry in your dream: This lets you know that it is time to be ambitious and to save money.
To give a hungry person something to eat: You will increase the amount of your belongings.

Hunter   To see one: Speculation or other risky ventures could cause serious loss.

Hunting   If you are hunting: You will be falsely accused of a wrong.
                         To be invited to a hunting trip: You have solved a puzzle. A relative makes an important concession.

Hunting horn   To blow one: Inquisitiveness brings positive responses.

Hurricane   To witness one: Unexpected events can disrupt plans and create unusual losses.
                         To hear the roar of one: You are making your neighborhood sick of you because you are so nervous all the time.

Husband   Be open-minded with all the members of your family.

Husar   To see one: You will probably have to increase your workspeed or workload if you really want to reach your goal.

Hyacinth   To see this flower in your dream: You will receive gifts.

Hydra (sea serpent) To see one: You will have to talk with your enemies if you want to achieve peace.

Hydropathic treatment To receive: You don't often believe in what you say.

Hyena   To dream about this animal: You must watch your temper.

Hymns   To hear them: This is a reminder to turn to a decent, moral lifestyle.

Hypnosis   To be hypnotized in a dream: An influential person who wishes to remain anonymous will give your career a shot in the arm.

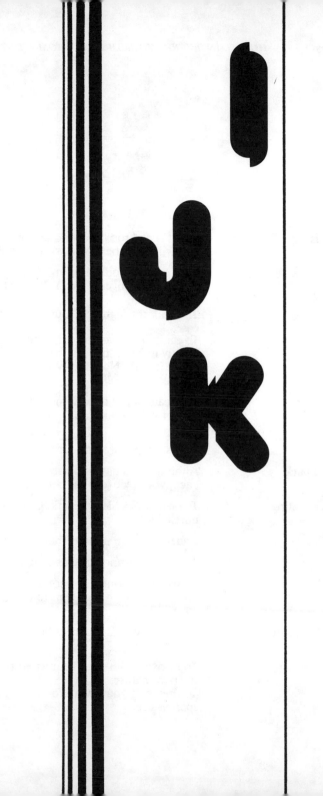

Ibis	Don't spend too much money on your children. You will likely be repaid with ingratitude.
Ice	To slip on it: You will hear bad news. To see snow-covered ice: You have to waive a claim. To break through ice: Your worries will be eased. To eat it: Take care of your strength. To buy it: Your love will be returned. To see it melt: Not all of your hopes will be fulfilled.
Iceberg	To dream about one: Someone will take advantage of your weakness.
Icicle	To see one: Go ahead and reach out for help; others are just waiting for you to ask for it.
Ice pack	Although you have suffered an emotional setback, your recovery has been remarkable.
Ice skating	To be at an ice skating rink: Circumstances are unreliable.
Idiot	Endeavor to be smarter than your enemies.
Idler	To see one: Annoyance and anger.
Idol	To see one: Influential people will be helpful and sympathetic with problems that you are trying to cope with.
Ill-humored	Your behavior is not at its best and will cause you trouble.
Illness	To recover from one: Your aspirations are not of the right nature. To dream of your own: You may enjoy a prosperous life.

Illumination
To see: You have an excess of mental energy which tends to make you hasty and impatient.

Imitation
To imitate someone: You will quarrel with an elderly woman.

Immodest
To be: A sense of drama constantly surrounds your activities.

Impatience
To have: You recognize what has to be done and you go ahead and do it.

Improper
If you have been living beyond your means, serious cutbacks are now required.

Incense
To smell it: You will finally get some peace.
To see it in a church: You are wise to invest in your health and lifestyle.

Index
To search for an address: Your project will not be successful.

Indians
To talk to them: What once seemed a lost cause is now revived and you are on a winning path.

Infantry
To see: Don't be so careless.
To join them: Don't let others in on your future plans.

Information
To give it: Good news is in store for you.

Ingratitude
To receive: The whole of the coming year will be favorable for you.

Inheritance
To receive one: A gift aimed at beautifying your surroundings could be on the way.

Injured
To be: This time luck is on your side.

Injury
To sustain one: Focus your energy on emotions, money and love.

Ink
To buy it: You will receive joyful tidings.
To see it: Someone will wrongfully accuse you.
To write with red ink: Read between the lines before you sign any contracts.
To write with green ink: There will be a big change in the near future.
To write with blue ink: Use your brain more often than your muscles.

Ink-pot
To dream about one means: You will become involved with the law.

Inlaid work   Many different things are turning out well for you.

Inn   To see one: Important business negotiations could make travel imperative.

Insane   To see others: Take better care of your health.

Inscription   To read one: A pecuniary loss occurs because you are too credulous.

Insects   To see them: What was once a pleasure for you could turn into a burden.
                         To be stung by one: Someone will cheat you.
                         To try to catch them: You have a great money gain.

Insinuate   You should be more diplomatic.

Instruction   To be taught: An association with intelligent persons.
                         To advise someone of a better lifestyle: Your well intended plans will come through, but not without some difficulties.

Instrument   To hear a musical one: A friend will spend his next vacation with you.

Insult   To be offended: You will lose someone whom you hold very dear.
                         To offend someone: This is a warning to watch your bad disposition.

Interpreter   To be one: You may have a good chance for success if you try to sort out your financial problems.

Intestine   To see them: You may feel uncomfortable.
                         To wash animals' intestines: Your efforts will not be rewarded.

Intoxication   To see someone in this state: A health problem could cause a financial burden.
                         To be intoxicated: Good news concerning your business.

Intrigue   Transform idealism into real action.

Inundation   To see one: You are frustrated and not in any mood to deal with domestic problems.

Invention   To invent something: If you play, you will definitely win some money.

Invitation   To get one: You may be strongly attracted to a newcomer.

Iron   To see melted iron: Try to finish your project as soon as possible and it will bring you profit.
To work with it: Someone offers you support that they do not really intend to give.
To be hurt by it. Misery.

Ironing   To do: A crowd of happy people will visit soon.

Island   To dream about a dull one: You will lose your fortune.
To be on one: You may soon have a financial breakthrough.

Itch   To have one: Put more effort into family entertainment.

Ivory   To dream about it indicates that you may have need to see a dentist.

Ivy   To see climbing ivy: Your mate or partner will understand you following a candid conversation.
To see poison ivy: You receive an important message from one confined to a hospital bed.
To plant ivy: You will find yourself in the right place at a crucial moment.

Jackdaw   To hear one crow: An accident may occur if you allow your mind to wander.

Jaguar   Creative enterprises are especially favorable at this time.

Jam   To eat it: A thorough knowledge of your diet would prove to be of great benefit.

Janitor   To see one: Difficulties with a neighbor could arise.

Jars	To buy them: Your budget is well-balanced. To see broken ones: Forewarns of poverty. To see full ones: Foretells success.
Jasmin	An unexpected visitor will delight you.
Jasper	To see: A valuable idea is the result of a conversation.
Jaundice	To have it: Slow down; you need some rest.
Javelin	To see or to throw one: Enemies and hatred. To be wounded by one: You may lose a lawsuit.
Jaws	Of a beast: It is better to discuss your failures than it is to conceal them.
Jay-bird	To see one flying: Make the best possible use of your invention.
Jealousy	You will learn more by first-hand experience with others than you possibly could from a book.
Jets of flame	To see them: A good idea will bring you profit.
Jewellery	To see: You will encounter difficulty doing business with people in far away places. To have some: Somebody will try to steal from you. To wear some: Loss of money is imminent. Made of pearls: Satisfaction in old age. Made of silver: Displeasure and illness. Made of gold: Don't be quite so outspoken.
Job	To look for one: If you are planning a trip by car, make absolutely sure that the car is in good shape. If you find one: Your next vacation will be significant.
Jockey	On horseback: A change in residence is possible.
Joke	You will marry a foreign person.
Joker	What had been lost for a long time may be recovered.
Journey	In an airplane: Barriers block the way to success. In a vehicle: More money will come your way. With company: Your income may shrink.
Judge	To see one: Reliable people surround you.

Judgement   To hear one: Be aware of possible damage.

Jug   To see one: Foretells an engagement or a marriage.
To break one: Those of you who are engaged should find a lifetime of happiness.

Juggler   To see yourself as one: You are surrounded by people who are only interested in your material worth.
To see one: Care is needed, but try not to overdo it.

Juice   From berries: Your illness will worsen.

Jump   You will be troubled by grief.

Jumping-jack   To see one: Expect to try much harder, but don't be surprised if your increased efforts are not rewarded financially.

June bugs   To catch them: Because of your kindness you will acquire many good friends.

Juniper   To see: You learn a hidden secret.

Junk-room   To see one: You will find hidden treasures.

Jury   Follow your instincts when handling money.

Kangaroo   To see one in a zoo: New contacts can provide you with useful information.

Kernels   To eat them: It appears that you will soon be out celebrating something.

Kettle   To see water boiling in one: Try to make the lives of others a bit easier for them.

Kettledrum   To hear one: You will lose your basic rights.

Key   To find one: You will rid yourself of a rival.
To have one in your hand: After a long, hard battle, you will reach your goal.

To fabricate one: Someone will disrupt your lifestyle.

To lose one: You are in for a big surprise.

Key-ring   You are soft-hearted. Someone will take advantage of you.

Kid   To see one: You will be blessed with many children.

Kidnap   To be kidnapped: Don't pay any attention to the suggestions of friends, no matter how sincere they may be.

To kidnap other people: Time may be against you, but you must decide whether or not to get married.

Kidnapper   To dream about one: Because your wounds have healed, it is safe to have confidence in your future. The outlook is good.

Kidneys   If you dream about your kidneys, your health will be good.

Kill   To kill somebody: You will overcome a great danger.

To kill someone with a gun: Grief and apprehension.

To see a defenseless person get killed: Friends you thought you could trust disappoint you with their unreliability.

Kindergarten   To see one: Your avarice will be your downfall.

Kiss   To kiss a girl: Stick to your present course of action.

To receive one: You are lucky that nobody knows about your secret.

To steal one: Your worries are over, but this is no excuse for arrogance.

Kitchen   To be in your own: Kindness costs you nothing but pays well. Use it.

Kite   To see one in the sky: This is a symbol of rising and falling plans, so it is best not to put too much confidence in your ideas.

Kitten   To see one: You are on the brink of giving in to temptation.

Knacker   To see one: Your mate or partner could bring you some unexpected good luck.

Knapsack	To carry one on your back: People will try to make a fool of you at a party.
Knee	To have a swollen one: You have good thoughts but don't listen to other people enough. To see an injured one: Avoid a quarrel with a friend.
Kneeling	In front of others: Have more confidence in yourself.
Knick-knacks	To buy them: You suffer a pecuniary loss.
Knife	To use one: Unexpected wealth. Somebody will calumniate you for wrong doings.
Knight	To see him in a suit of armor: Don't get involved in a love affair right now.
Knighthood	To be elevated into: Be aware of the small print. Your security is at stake.
Knitting	To see yourself knitting in a dream means: This is a favorable time for making a special effort to improve your health.
Knob	To change one on your door: Do not divulge secrets connected with your job to strangers.
Knock down	To see someone be knocked down: There may be a dispute with your employer.
Knocking	Don't start anything you're not absolutely positive you can finish.
Knots	To tie one: The letter you are waiting for will not arrive by mail. To untie one: Your wishes will come true. To see many of them: Any business that can be transacted today will most likely prove to be profitable.
Knuckles	To see your own: Don't drop in unexpectedly on people you haven't seen for some time.

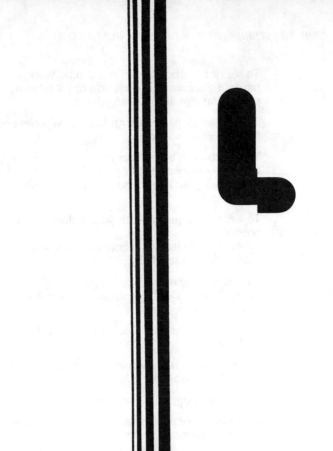

Label

To see or to stick a label: You should work harder to accomplish what you think other people at your age have already done.

Labor pains

To have labor pains in your dream: Worries and fear will enter your life.

Labryinth

To go astray in one: Misery and apprehension do not go away as fast as you wish they would. Don't lose your confidence, everything will work out.

Lace

To wear it: A quarrel with your fellow workers is possible.
To wear white lace: It is better to save some money than none at all.

Lacquer

To see: Beware of strange people.
To work with: Don't get upset over small matters.

Ladies

Seeing a get-together: Don't make promises you can't keep.

Ladies society

To be involved in a club: Accept people for who they are, not who you want them to be.

Ladle

A couraging sign for your venture.

Lady

To see or to try and contact her: This is a sign of delight in the near future.

Lady visitor

Be ready for a variety of sensations.

Lagoon

To see one: Be careful when boating, swimming or fishing.

Lake

To fish in one: You will meet a dynamic, creative individual who will help you realize your own potential.
A calm lake: People will help you if you are having problems with work.
Stormy: You will escape a dangerous situation.

Lakei

To see or speak to one: Work hard and you will find that you are in the right place at the right time.

Lamb

To see in a pasture: Do not let a negative attitude undo all the success you have achieved lately.
A white one: Your innocence will be proven.
A black one: Protect your reputation - be discreet.

To see a lost one: Your own stupidity will cause you to suffer a loss.

Lament To hear: You will receive a gift of extraordinary value.

Lamp To turn one on: You will give very important advice to a friend.
To turn one off: Don't destroy others hopes.
To see one: Try to get your work in order now.
To carry one: Your love life will improve if you have more confidence in yourself.

Lance To carry one: Soon it will be the opposite - your opponent will ask for harmony.

Land To see it from the ocean: Current trends are working in your favor.
To see it from the plane: Do not allow your hard earned cash to be wasted away.

Landlord To see or speak to one: If you cut back on unnecessary spending, you will be able to make some valuable savings.

Lantern To see one: Somebody is trying to harm you, but you are aware of it. You will be able to defend yourself.
To light one: You will receive an invitation, but avoid attending the function.
Extinguish: Avoid making any secret agreements.

Lap To sit on somebody's: Don't expose yourself to danger.

Larbord Be on a ship or see the side: You will travel abroad.

Lard Hot: Hopeful future.

Lark To hear one sing: True love will make you very happy but, nevertheless, take care of yourself.
To see one: Be cautious in business transactions.

Larkspur To pick: Be very careful when agreeing to do something.
This also means happiness is forthcoming.

Larva To see: A close friend lies to you.

Lasso To throw one: Refuse to allow yourself to be

pressured into making decisions. Allow plenty of time to think things over.

Lathe To see or handle one: Your efforts will be not as successful as you think they will be.

Laughing Yourself: Consider what you want to do carefully, then proceed to do it.
To hear: Your overzealousness makes you look ridiculous.

Laundress To see one at work: Recent family budget discussions bear fruit.

Laundry To see: Is not a very good omen.
To work with or in a laundry: Somebody who has hurt your feelings very badly will apologize to you.

Laurel To see one: You have a very good opportunity to improve your position.

Lavatory To be in one: You have no reason to be ashamed.
To repair: The hatred directed toward you originates from your side of the family.

Lavender To see or smell it: Don't have any fear; luck is with you.

Lawnmower To hear the motor of or work with one: You will be embarrassed.

Lawsuit To be involved in one: You can depend on your spouse.
To witness one: Do not make any hasty decisions which you could regret in the future.

Lawyer To see one: Authoritative figures will make your life difficult.
To speak to a lawyer: Somebody is observing you.
To listen to one: You will find yourself in bad company.

Lead To pour lead: Watch for false friends who tell lies and are fraudulent.
To see or have lead in your surroundings: Do not sign anything that would commit you too far ahead in the future.
To see a lead bullet: Don't get involved in adventures.

Learn

You are unbelievably careful but, nevertheless, a love affair will change something in your life.

Leaseholder

To see one: Don't let your imagination run away with you.
To be one: A loss in the near future.

Leather

To see: The path you are following right now is a very difficult one.
To touch or wear: Avoid all disputes.

Leaves

Green: Good fortune could come your way in business.
Colored: Ask your parents if you can be of any help to them.
If you see them falling down: Do not stop any activities. If you stay in the race you will be successful.
Withered: Health and happiness.

Ledger

To read or write in it: You will enter a worrisome period unless you not change your mind about something.

Legs

To see pretty legs: This means luck and health are imminent. It also means a friend will get married very soon.
To look at your own legs in a dream: Exercise is good for you. Think about it.
You break one of your legs in a dream: Shame and disgrace in the business community.
To see one amputated: Loss of a good friend.
To see skinny or sick legs: Treachery from friends.
If you see people walking and only see the legs: You will make a fortune during your lifetime.

Lemonade

To drink: Emphasis on friends' hopes and a reunion with a family member.

Lemons

To see them grow on a tree: You should devote more time to your personal affairs and hobbies.
To squeeze one or to see somebody else doing it: Be aware of fraudulent people.
If you see green ones: Somebody has lied to you.

Lentil

To eat: Pleasurable activities will not live up to your expectations.

Leopard

To see one behind bars: Take more time to appreciate knowledge in general.

To be attacked by one: Gossip and apprehension.

Letter

If you receive one in a dream: The attention paid to you by a member of the opposite sex will be extremely flattering and very welcome.
To write one: You may be able to get a tricky tax matter straightened out satisfactorily.
A letter torn to pieces: You will be seriously insulted.
To seal one: Have patience with your children.

Letter card

To get one: Your laziness will cause you trouble.

Letter of credit

To see or receive one: Your work will be successful.

Lettuce

To eat it: Means sickness.
To see it: The time you spent on one of your family members was nothing but a wasted effort.
To buy: Things would be better if you cared more about yourself.

Lever

To work with one: Soon you will overcome your difficulties.

Library

To be in one: If you would like to reach your goal, make sure your actions are proper, and fear no one.

License

To receive: A lawsuit turns out to be prosperous.

Lick

To see yourself licking something: Be aware of flatterers - they may try to swindle money from you.
To get licked by somebody or by an animal: Try to be very polite to your neighbors, otherwise, they may trick you.

Licorice

To buy it: Your appearance is successful.

Lie

If you lie somewhere in a dream: Sharing your spare time with others, especially elderly people, will prove to be very advantageous for you.
If you lie on stones or rocks: Poverty and worries.

Lie

To tell somebody a lie: Beware - you are on the verge of suffering a great loss.
Somebody is lying to you: In the immediate

future you will have the opportunity to lead
your life as you please.

Lifeboat
To see or be in one: Honor and respect. This
also means that you will have good luck in
business.

Light
To see light from a great distance: Your past ex-
periences have taught you valuable shortcuts.
To see: Pleasure comes from discerning clues.

Lighter
To use one: Don't give up the project you are
working on.

Lighthouse
To see one: At social gatherings you are seldom
unnoticed by members of the opposite sex.

Lightning
To see lightning strike your house: If you are
wealthy it means loss. If you are poor, it means
a more pleasant time in the future.
If thunder is following lightning it is a warning
to discontinue and give in to an undesirable
disposition.

Lily
To pick one: Listen to what your partner or
spouse has to say.
To pick white ones: Creative work can produce
more definitive results.

Lily of the valley
To see or to pick: You will receive gifts from nice
people.

Limb
To see yourself lose one: You will be freed from
an unpleasant situation.
To see disfigured limbs: Don't get into a panic
over a situation which you cannot change.

Lime tree
To see: If you know deep down that you have
been in the wrong over some important issue,
admit it.
In bloom: Unexpected good news.

Lime twig
To see or touch one: There is a strong possibility
of deception or fraud.

Limp
To see yourself limp or lame: Your plans will be
temporarily halted.
To see others limp: Your business is
disorganized.

Linen
To see fine linen: You should give yourself credit
because of your thriftiness.

To touch rough linen: Hard work brings its own rewards.
To see it very clean: Good health.
To see it dirty: Quarrels.

Linseed   It would be unwise to ignore minor ailments.

Lion   To tame one: You have a friend in a critical situation.
To hear one roar: A serious conflict with relatives may develop.
To be chased by one: You get well. Your sickness is not life-threatening.
To kill one: Don't play the hero. It won't help anyone.
To play with a lion or to see lion cubs in a dream: Now is a very advantageous time to take a vacation.
To shoot one: Don't ruin your luck.
To be overpowered by a lion: Your enemies will give you a chance for reconciliation.
To see a lion chasing another animal: Make an effort to help a needy friend.
To see one caged: Your enemies are not strong enough to do you any harm.
To see one furious: Your knowledge is your best weapon.
To see one in the desert: Try to communicate more with your neighbors. It will give you peace and relaxation.

Lips   To see: You strike it lucky with someone you love.

Liquor   To drink it: Good fortune ahead of you.
To buy it: Don't be thoughtless.
To give it away: You should be aware of bad influences on your children.

Listen   At a door: Be on the alert - somebody could seduce you.
In the open wilderness: You learn something that will worry you.
In a house: If you do not change your lifestyle, you will someday be lonely.

Liver   To eat it: Your health is excellent.

Livery   To see one: If you have difficulties concentrating at work, take a day off. If you don't, you are taking a chance of having an accident.

Lizard

If you kill a lizard in a dream: Somebody is trying to pull the rug out from under your feet.
To see one: You will have much amusement within the next few days.

Load

To carry one: They will point the suspicion at you.
To drop one: Employment affairs may bring increased workloads.

Loading

If you are loading something in a dream: There is a very good chance that you will get rich.

Loan

To receive a loan: You will take over a responsibility.
To make a loan: Don't be so eager to make a new start. It is better to hold your horses for the time being.
To repay a loan: You should beware of fire.

Lobsters

To eat or see them: This is a reminder to go ahead and finish the project you had started.

Lock

If you keep an open mind, you will be successful.

Locked in

To be: Your fears are groundless. Offer resistance to your inner fiend.
To become: Familiarize yourself with the views of those who do not necessarily agree with you.

Locksmith

To see one in your dream: If you are young you should think about learning a trade. Also, this dream reminds elderly people to save their money.

Log

To see one: Beware and ignore idle gossip.

Look at and contemplate

To gaze at: You will be pitied after an accident.

Loop

To see one: You should think more economically.

Lord's Prayer

To pray: Your worries will soon fade away.
To hear somebody praying: You will achieve greater independence and will be freed from burden which had retarded your progress.
To hear children pray: Your trust in God will be rewarded.

Lord's Supper

To partake of the Lord's Supper: Is a forewarning of grief in the family.

Deliver the Lord's Supper: You will save a person from death.

Lose
If you lose something in a dream: You will have luck and will gain in business.

Lot
You see or own one: You will lose part of your wealth.

Lottery ticket
To buy one: You will receive a very good offer.
To find one: If you are in possession of one, you will win.

Loudspeaker
To see one: Think more about your work. It is the only channel for success.

Lounge
Overseas travel becomes a distinct possibility.

Louse
To have lice: Luck will always be with you.
To see one: Unexpected money will come your way.
If you see large lice in a dream: An unbelievable success.

Love affair
To have one in a dream: You will be able to resolve a difference of opinion that took place with someone in another city.

Lover
You should be cautious.

Love-sick
To be in a dream: A very good year is ahead of you.

Low tide
Your current situation is unstable.

Luck
If you experience luck in your love life or in gambling: Postpone any new purchases for the time being.

Luggage
To see it: Don't do unlawful things.
To buy it: It will be better to postpone a trip.
To carry it: Save some money for a rainy day.

Lumber
To see it: You will receive help from unexpected sources.
To work with it. Don't refuse an offer.

Lunatics
To see them: Grief for lovers.

Lunch
Soon you will be invited to a party.

Lute
To play one: You should be able to have a good time socially and forget all about your problems at work.

	To see one: Show your wife that you love her.
Luxury	You must take care with your eating habits.
Lye	To work with: Take your time and don't rush things.
Lying in state	To see somebody: Sadness.
Lynx	To see one: Your current situation requires outside help.
Lyre	Don't change your goal from one day to the other.

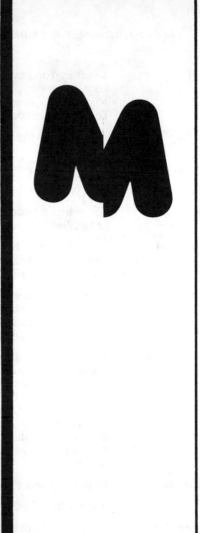

Macaroni

To eat it: You have a happy home life. Try to keep it that way.
To cook it: You are slipping into debt.
To see it: A barrier to your proposition.

Machine gun

To see one: After many rainy days the sun will shine again.
To handle one: You will not get the support that you had been hoping for from either your family or your friends.

Madonna

To see her in your dream: Your expectations will be fulfilled by your spouse.

Magazine (gun)

To see it empty: News from afar is forthcoming.
To see it full: A long journey ahead of you with negative implications.

Magician

To see one on a stage performing: Small quarrels make you nervous. Overlook them.
To be one yourself: You should complete that important assignment.

Magistrate's office

To dream about this office: Trouble and grief will come your way.
To see a staff member of: Someone is interfering in your affairs.
To become a staff member of: You triumph over your enemy.
Be lost in the building of: It would be all too easy to give way to lethargy, but you must not give in.

Magnanimous

To be in a dream: A jail term may be in sight.

Magnet

A good friend will contact you.

Magnifying glass

To look through or handle one: Do not go along with the speculative propositions of associates. They will only lead to loss for you.

Magpie

To see one: Hide your valuables.

Mahogany

To see it in your dream: Take care of your belongings. Make repairs before it is too late.

Maid

To have one working for you in a dream: You are lucky enough to have a good sense of humor.

Maid of honor

To see or be one yourself: Something is following you. Try to find out what and get rid of it.

Mailman   To see one: You will receive a letter you have
                    waited a long time for.
                    To speak to one: News from next of kin is com-
                    ing.
                    To see a mailman from a distance: You will
                    receive a registered letter containing good news.

Main floor   To have an apartment on: A pleasant life is
                    ahead of you.

Make-up   In front of a mirror: Fight for your life.

Mallet   To see or work with one: You will receive money
                    or a nice gift.

Man   For a woman to see one: Be aware of someone
                    who will dominate you.
                    To see an old man in your dream: Be more can-
                    did with your children.
                    For a young woman to see men: A man will ask
                    you to marry him.
                    For a man seeing a man or many men: Liberate
                    yourself from bad influences.

Man-of-war   To see one: You will have a sad experience.
                    To touch one: Trouble with your health.

Mandarin   You should care more about your knowledge.

Manege (school for You will receive an invitation.
horsemanship)
Manger   To see or fill one: You must on no account pay
                    more than your fair share simply to keep peace.
                    Bankers will not be as helpful as you would like.

Manner   To see a bad mannered person: Don't mislead
                    yourself about your financial situation.

Manure   To see it: Benefits in your occupation.
                    To smell it: Success in everything.
                    Loaded on a truck: Unexpected luck.
                    To collect it: Your excellent ideas are as good as
                    gold.

Manuscript   To read one: You take too much interest in other
                    people.
                    To write one: Most of your dreams will come
                    true.
                    You send one to a publisher: Give up your
                    hopes. Other objects are taking up too much of
                    your time.

Map
To study: If possible, avoid making a journey.

Maple leaf or the Canadian flag
You will live comfortably if you stay in your homeland.

Marble
To see: You will have conflicts with relatives.
To polish marble: This is a sign of misfortune.
To see it broken: Stay on the straight and narrow path.

Marble statue
To see one: You will lose a good friend.

Marching
If you have to: You may soon be entering partnership with a close friend.
You see somebody else marching: The only way to improve your financial situation is through work that you can handle unaided by others.

Margarine
To see or eat it: Good times won't last forever.

Marigolds
To see or to pick them: Bad days will be over soon.
For farmers it foretells good crops.

Mariner
To be one: You will have a surprise.
To see one: Inheritance.

Market
To see: Your business will improve.
To walk across: Stick to the rules at your place of employment.

Marmot
To see or have: Your old age is free of worries.

Marriage
To get: Now is the time to work hard to have your ideas accepted to make desired changes.
To separate: Arguments may easily become serious if you insist upon having your own way.

Married
To be: Mutual love is real in your marriage.

Marrow bone
Wealth for you and your family.

Marzipan
To eat: Keep your children at home or they will have bad luck.

Mask
To wear one: Don't disappoint a good friend.
To see one: Somebody is likely to defraud and disappoint you.
To see others wearing a mask: Do not lend money to anyone unless you have written guarantees as to when you will be paid back.

Masonic lodge
To be a member of: Emotions are as vast as the

	ocean, yet in the pain of confusion there is hope in the secrets of one's own heart.
Masquerade	To see one: A couple of visitors will surprise you over the next few days.
Mass	To attend one: Your success is without barriers.
Mast	To see one: Your salary will increase.
Master builder	At a scaffold: Danger is surrounding you; be extra careful.
Mat	To see or lie on one: Somebody wants to destroy your luck.
Matches	Take care of your health.
Matron	You will die a natural death.
Mattress	To see a new one: Happiness and luck. To see an old one: Misfortune through unfaithfulness.
Mausoleum	To be in: Somebody will try to ruin your reputation. To see one: Sickness in your family.
May bowl (punch)	To drink it: Beware of wheedlers.
Mayor	If you are a mayor in a dream: People will honor you.
Meal	Of meat: Means good luck. From flour: Means sickness.
Measles	To have: Your pleasures will increase.
Measure	Something: You are surrounded by evil people.
Meat	To give it to a dog: People despise you. To see it roasted: This is a sign of a bad harvest. To buy it: You will be involved in a quarrel. To eat it raw: Financial support comes from an unexpected source. Fetid meat: You resolve a dilemma and perceive hidden motives.
Medal	To receive one: You will be able to replace your loss.
Medicine	Bitter: Your enemies will suppress you. To give it to someone: Mishaps and worries will be followed by good times.

Medium   To see: You are under a bad influence.

Medlar   If you see one in your dream: You will be disappointed in your hopes.

Meet   To meet friends or other welcome persons in your dream: A mishap in your undertaking. To meet someone: A word of warning - do not speculate.

Meeting   To attend one: Beware - you are in a dangerous situation.

Megaphone   To see or to use one in a dream: You won't get any answer to the question you ask just yet.

Melancholy   To feel: Delight and enjoyment.

Melon   To see or eat one in a dream: Do not force yourself in to a troublesome situation.

Memorial   To see one: Be more sympathetic with others.

Menagerie   To see one: Whatever may happen, you will reach your goal.

Mending   To repair something: Enrich your knowledge by reading.

Mentally ill   To be: Avoid becoming involved with the debts of others. To see mentally ill people in a dream: There will be arguments and serious disagreements with your associates.

Merchandise   To buy: Disturbances may occur at home.

Merchant   To see or speak to one: A big money gain is very possible.

Mercury   Deceitful people surround you.

Mercy   To have in a dream: Don't complain about your situation. It could be worse.

Messenger   To see one walking or to send one off: The dreamer will probably receive unpleasant news in the next few days. To see yourself as a messenger: Someone will tell you an important secret, one which you will have to honor. If you speak to a messenger for a long time: Avoid making impulsive decisions.

Meteor	If you see one in your dream: An unexpected short period of good luck.
Meteorite	If you see many of them: Your biggest wish will come true.
Metric measure	To see or work with one in a dream: You will be involved in a court case.
Microscope	To see or work with one: Somebody will try to trick you.
Midget	To see one: What you have in mind to do will be successful. To speak to one: You are not the only one who is intelligent.
Midnight	To witness: Blame yourself for the unpleasant things that happen to you.
Mid-summer festival	To attend one: Make your decision very carefully and you will have success.
Midwife	To see or speak to her: You can make a fortune, but you may lose it if you are not clever.
Mignonette	To pick: You have luck in business.
Migration	You see people in your dream: You can accomplish a lot if you really apply yourself.
Milestone	To see: Time is favorable for short trips and new contacts are the result. To pass by: You will reach the object of your desire.
Military exercise	To see one: A good opportunity for a new career is coming up.
Military hospital	To see one: Try to have more control over your passions.
Milk	To buy it: Enjoyment for you. To spill it: Save your money. To drink: Your health is likely to improve greatly.
Milking cow	To see one: A new friendship is making your life bright.
Milk jug	To see or handle one: You will have unexpected visitors.

Mill
To see or work in one: Your fortune will multiply.

Miller
To see one at work: Hard work brings its own rewards.

Mill stone
If you see one in your dream: Death in your surroundings.

Mill-wheel
To see one: You will improve your fortune, but be aware of envious kin.
To hear one: You will be disappointed of friends.

Mine
To work in one: It is time for you to give considerable thought to your future economic security.
To visit one: Jobs that you begin now may never be brought to their successful conclusions.

Minerals
To collect: Your knowledge is too sparse for the things which you like to do.

Mint money
To see: It is worth giving thought to how easily we are deceived.

Miracle
If you see a miracle in a dream: Place more emphasis on getting your personal life organized.

Mirror
To look in one: Expansion of your business.

Miscalculate
In a dream: Do what you can to establish better lines of communication.

Miser
To see one: You must not coerce people into acting against their better judgment.

Misery
To be in: Your present situation is good, but it is wise to think about your future.
To see somebody else in misery: A big change will occur during your absence.

Missionary
To see or to be one: Try to be good to other people.

Mistletoe
To see it in a dream: This is a good omen.

Misunderstanding
To have some in a dream: Follow your instincts and don't listen to others.

Mites
To have: Jealousy will disrupt your happiness.

Mocked
To be: Maintain a low profile and permit others to express their opinions.

Mockery   To witness: Somebody will soon surprise you.

Mocking-bird   To hear one: You will have a small loss but through it, you will be lucky.

Model   To be one: Your dignity is in question.
                     To see a model in your dream: Don't believe in extravagant promises.

Mole   To see one: You are being unfairly criticized - defend yourself.

Monastery   To go into one: Your church needs you.
                     To see one: Some volunteer work will be beneficial to you. It will give your life new direction and purpose.

Money   To find: You are a lucky person in life not only in your dreams.
                     To lose: Watch the people you work with.
                     To count: Small upset will bring you profit.

Money-box   To see one: Your lifestyle will undergo transformation.

Money purse   To have an empty one: Don't lose your temper in front of other people.
                     To have a full money purse in a dream: A good omen.

Monk   To see one: Poverty may come over you.

Monkey   To see one or more: Watch out for crooks.
                     To see one climbing: An enemy is trying to bring you down.
                     To tease them: You will thoughtlessly hurt a friend.
                     To see monkeys dance: You will make a prosperous decision.
                     To kill a monkey: You will have to endure harsh times.
                     To see a long tailed monkey: Somebody will try to get you in trouble with the authorities.
                     If a monkey tries to bite you in a dream: Someone is trying to steal your good money-making idea.

Monogram   To see or to embroider one: Your children give you cause to worry.

Monster   To see one: Have faith in your destiny.

To slay one: A threatening disaster may come over you.

Monument
To see a tall, beautiful monument: This signifies an honorable career ahead. Don't misuse it.
To set one up: Through memories your achievements live on.
To see an old one: Secrecy is recommended while handling financial matters.

Moon
To see it: You will meet a very nice person.
To see a half moon: A well-known personality will die.
Full moon: You will reach your goal.
Moon with clouds: Strange things happen in your family.
With a circle: You and your loved one should openly discuss differences that you have been brushing under the carpet.
To see a rising moon: Tragedy in love or marriage.
To see a new moon: Somebody will try to mislead you.

Moorland
To see it dried up: Surreal happenings.
To see it pretty and green: Your hopes did not let you down.
To see it in bloom: Something will change for the better.

Morning aurora
Soon your pain will be over.

Morning star
You see one in your dream: Your good luck is short lived.

Moral philosophy
Somebody speaks to you or you read about it: You did nothing wrong. You can even be proud of your actions. You are correct in most of your decisions.

Morass
After many hard days of work you will have success.

Mortgage
To give: Miserable times ahead of you.
To take: You must be more ambitious to reach your goal.

Mosquito
To see one or get hurt by one: Don't pay any attention to the rumor about your colleague.
To kill one: You could not keep a secret.

Moss	To rest on it: Your health is good. To see it green: Long life. To pick it: If you are a farmer you will have a good crop. To hold it in your hands: Wealth is on your side.
Motel	To see one: You should think about taking a vacation. To check in or out of one: If you leave your home, lock your doors properly to avoid disappointment when you return.
Mother	If you see your mother in a dream: This always is a good omen. In the future you will have happiness, prosperity and good luck. To speak with your mother in a dream: Don't pay any attention to the rumors of strangers.
Mother-in-law	To see or talk to her: You will have luck in your business transactions.
Mother-of-pearl	To buy it: Your behavior is hard to understand. Try to change it. To have some: Face danger head on.
Moths	To have them: You should exercise more to keep you young and healthy. To see them: Somebody will call you to account for your actions.
Motion	To see yourself in motion: Unnecessary work. Being in a garden: Avoid misunderstandings. In a house: You will make valuable connections.
Motive	To be annoyed: Don't take everything so seriously.
Motorboat	To see or to drive one: Take time to work things out, otherwise you may run into big trouble. To buy one: Your wish will be realized.
Motto	To read one: Your expectations are not so high after all.
Mould	To see one in your dream: Don't look for protection from people who take advantage of you.
Moulding	To work with: To deal in real estate is not profitable right now. To see one or more: Any work done on your property can only increase its value.

Mountain	To climb one: You will cvercome your worries. To climb down one: Your wish won't come true. To see them at a far distance: Your hopes will be fulfilled. With snow on top: A pleasant journey is ahead of you. If you see a mountain chain in a dream: You speak in an awkward manner to people. It may harm you socially.
Mountain dwellers	To see them at work: Through work you will accomplish your goals, luck and well-being. To see one: You have some happy idle moments.
Mourning	Yourself in a dream: It is a sign that you should change your behavior and that you must try to get along better with other people. To see other people mourning in your dream: Hypocritical people will try to influence you.
Mourning dress	To wear: Harmony will replace dissension within the family circle. If you see strange people wearing mourning dress in your dream: It is a bad omen.
Mouse	To hear the squeak of one: Be on the alert for your belongings. To see one: Losses and quarrels in your family. To see a white one or many of them: Your married life will be good and your harmony will bring you wealth.
Mouth	To see a big one: Wealth through inheritance. A small one: Don't play with your luck.
Moustache	Disadvantages in the near future.
Move	To move from a house or apartment: Bad news. To help someone moving: A financial dilemma is on the brink of being resolved.
Moved	Being aware of somebody who has moved away: Soon you will get happy news from far places.
Movie	To see one: Seize every opportunity to show influential people your diverse talents.
Moving in	Someplace yourself: Friends have been waiting a long time for an invitation. To see people moving in: Don't waste time on people with no manners.

Mud	Watch out for unscrupulous and unreliable people.
Muff	Bad times are ahead of you.
Mug	To see one: Good news. To drink out of it: First impressions are likely to be correct.
Mulberries	Your harvest will be abundant.
Murder	To commit: Try to go a straight way and don't become involved in uncertain things. Otherwise, you may regret it for a long time. To see somebody commit murder: Some envious people would like to see you miserable.
Murderer	If you see one in your dream: Somebody is trying to give you a bad name.
Muse	If science is your hobby, you have a good chance of making it your business.
Museum	To visit one: Practical knowledge makes your job much easier than it is for the average person.
Mushrooms	To see them: Somebody will favor and promote you. To eat them: You will reach an old age.
Music	To hear it: You are worried, and someone comforts you.
Musical notes	To see them: Your hopes will be fulfilled.
Muskrat	To see one or hold one in your hand: Happiness and honor.
Musky smell	You are under false suspicion.
Mute	To be: You have a sick mind. To see somebody as mute: Don't talk so much about your health problems to other people. They don't want to hear about them.
Muzzle	Don't get involved in gossip.
Myrmidon	Your sickness will be over soon.
Myrtle	Your spouse respects and loves you very much. Be more dependable.

Nails	To drive them in: Your proposal is a good one. To find them: Poverty comes to your home. To see long ones: You can expect help.
Naked	To be: Death in your neighborhood.
Name	To write one: Take care of a lawsuit. To hear your own: Somebody will ask you for advice. To see your own name written: You have given your word to a friend. Keep it.
Napkin	You destroy your own luck.
Nasty	To be: You will visit a sick person.
Native	To see one: Use tact to resolve a difficult problem with employees.
Nausea	To feel: Don't be quite so extravagant.
Navel	To see one: Bad luck is ahead of you.
Navy	Your upcoming journey will be interrupted.
Neck	To wash your own: Good health. To have a swollen one: Happiness. To break your own: Warning of danger. To see your own: Honor and dignity. To see the neck of another person: Warning of foolhardiness.
Necklace	To wear one made of gold or silver: Good luck in love and entertainment. To wear one made of coral: Impulsive moves must be avoided. To buy one: Romance can be happy but sudden events can be upsetting.
Necktie	To see or wear one: Family happiness.
Needles	To find: Have peace of mind. To get: You and your friends will be separated.
Negligee	Your husband is keeping secrets from you.
Negro	To see many: You are surrounded by friendly people. To see a female: Your difficulties will soon be over. To see a male: If you are more patient you will reach your goal. To see children: You will have a happy marriage.

Neighbors	To see or talk to them: Don't trust your people so much.
Nest	To see an empty one: You will be absent from your residence for a long time. To see one with birds or eggs in it: This is a very good omen.
Net	To fish with one: Don't be a wheeler - dealer. To see one: Don't do improper things.
Nettle	To pick: Take time to do things, don't hurry. To see or work with: Look at people closely.
News	To hear some: Don't hurry too much.
Newspaper	To buy one: To own property is more important to you than it is to the average individual. To read one: You have to make a decision involving a member of the opposite sex.
Niche	To sit in one: Luck with your children and marriages.
Nickel watch	To see or wear one: You have good thoughts, but don't listen too much to your spouse.
Night	A dark one: Quarrels with relatives. A clear one: You will have a long, pleasant life. A stormy one: Look for a better job.
Night bird	Be careful on the job and at home. There is danger of an accident.
Night cap	To wear one: You will soon be engaged.
Night chamber	To see one: Hostility in your neighborhood. To break one: Be wary of people who want you to part with your cash for speculative purpose. To use one: Romance will play a very important role in your life.
Night dew	To feel it on your body: You are in touch with false friends.
Nightingale	To see one: You take a rather broad view of the truth. To hear one: With tact you can avoid serious arguments. To catch one: Your engagement will be a very happy one.

Night lodging   To see: Prosperity in your old age.

Night watch   To see, to have, or to be one: Watch your domestic servants.

Nine   To see this number: A big success will occur.

Nitre   To buy or work with: For women it means a good time, for men it means disgrace.

Noise   To hear: Somebody will try to defraud you.
To make: Unforeseen circumstances may cause you to change your plans at the last moment.

Noodles   To make them: Somebody will help you at the right time.

Northern lights   To see them: Unexpected tidings bring you enjoyment.

Nose   A big one: You will have a good spouse.
A small one: Happiness and love.
A red one: Wealth and honor will be with you.

Nosebleed   Your health is very good.

Notary   To speak to one: Inheritance.
To see one: Now is not the right time to begin new projects.

Notebook   To have one: Don't be selfish: everybody wants to live.
To lose one: Don't be forgetful or you may have to pay.

Notice   To make one: Dishonor.

Novel   To write one: Grief and anxiety.

Numbers   If you dream that you see some numbers: Most of the time these are lucky numbers. When you wake up write them down. They may prove to be useful.

Nun   To see one: Make an effort to widen your circle of acquaintances.
To see more than one: You must try harder at work.
To be one yourself: A change of position.

Nunnery   To be in or see one: An unhappy secret love affair.

Nurse   To see one: Foretells sickness.

For a young woman seeing a nurse in a dream: Means that you will become a mother.
To be one yourself: There is nothing to be gained by creating a scene or insisting that others are being unreasonable.

Nursery governess   To be one yourself: You will be led into temptation.
To see one: You will obtain information which could be important to your health.

Nutmeg   To taste or use it: Avoid disputes between you and your spouse.

Nuts   To see them: Don't worry about the future.
To eat them: Don't be irritated.
To crack them open: Hard work is ahead of you.
To pick or to buy them: Unexpected luck.

Nymph   To be or to see one: Soon you will be a fiancé.

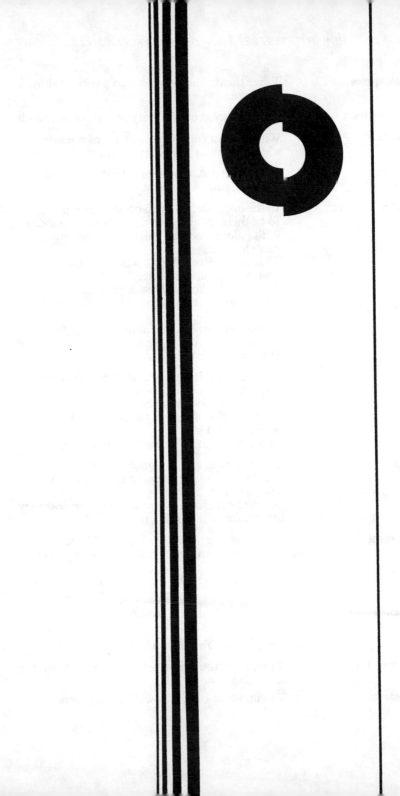

Oak apples   To see them: You may get into a very wealthy marriage.

Oak leaves   Now is a good opportunity to make new friends.

Oak tree   With leaves: You will be well rid of a burden which was not rightfully yours in the first place.

Oar   To steer one: A beautiful, relaxing vacation is ahead of you.

Oasis   To see one: Success in all of your enterprises.
                   To be there: Make your decision without delay.
                   With palm trees: You will regret your wrong move too late.
                   With water: Everything takes time - don't lose your courage and patience.
                   With camels: You will reach your goal.
                   With tourists: Be very careful in what you agree to.
                   Without water: You are able to survive.
                   To live in one: You will have to adapt to changes and unexpected developments.

Oath   To swear one: Be strong and don't allow others to intimidate you.
                   To see somebody swear one: You are on your way to performing a silly action. Think carefully before you do it.
                   To break an oath: Be ready for a quick change.

Oats   To see them in a field: Ignore prophets of gloom and doom, you are about to make a start in a new direction.
                   To make oat chaff: There will be an opportunity to increase your earning power.

Oatmeal   To prepare oatmeal: The kind of job that you are requested to perform will test your ingenuity.
                   To eat it: You will be promoted in your occupation.

Obelish   To see one: You have reason to be very satisfied with your business.

Oboe   To play one: You have a taste for art.

Observatory   To see one: You should enjoy the challenges that are facing you.

Obstacle   To jump over one: You will be disappointed.

Ocean	With waves: You will make a fortune in your business. To see the ocean calm: You will become engaged. To see the ocean turbulent: Observe your surroundings.
Ocean cruise	To take one: Delight and love.
Oculist	To be in his office: You seek justice for others, but often forget about yourself.
Odor	To be surrounded by: Someone you had been hoping to meet could be ill or on a vacation.
Offer	A trip could easily result in a complete waste of time and money.
Officials	To see any kind of official in uniform indicates unpleasant news is forthcoming. It also means that you are most likely never to marry.
Official robe	To see one: Maintain caution against burglars.
Officer	To be with one in an officers' club: There will be trouble in your married life for a few days.
Oil	To spread it on yourself: Past errors will be rectified. To work with it: You will recoup a loss and will be given a second chance. To see it burn: Influential people will be too wrapped up in other affairs to listen to you. To spill it: Try to heal rifts that have developed between you and an older relative.
Ointment	To buy it: Unhappy people seek your counsel. To apply it: Do everything within your means to improve your overall condition.
Olives	To eat them: Don't be quite so lavish. To remove them from a jar: The pleasure you experience will be fascinating, but dangerous.
Olive tree	In the near future you will accumulate a small profit.
Olympiad	To dream about the Olympic games tells you that you will soon make a social appearance.
Omelette	To prepare one: A family disagreement will be resolved.

	To serve one: You may have an unfair advantage over somebody.
One-way street	Unless much tact and diplomacy are used, arguments will develop.
Onion	Consider taking a keep-fit course to get yourself into better physical shape.
Onyx	Avoid allowing people to intrude into your life.
Opal	To mount one in a ring: People are praising your purity.
Opera	To be in an opera house: Don't be hard-hearted towards others.
Opera glass	To look through one: Your wishes will be fulfilled.
Operation	To undergo an operation: However minor they may appear, health problems should not be ignored.
Opium	To see it: Your intelligence keeps you out of trouble.
Oranges	To squeeze the juice out of: You will have lover's grief. To eat them: You have great desire for a forbidden pleasure. To buy them: You will be engaged with new relationships. To see them growing on a tree: One of your friends is hiding his true nature from you. To pick them: You will only attain success in a foreign country.
Orangutan	To dream about one: You may run into someone with whom you lost touch a long time ago.
Orator	To listen to one: You should bring the idealistic and romantic elements of your nature out into the open.
Orchard	To see one: You will soon visit your girl friend or boy friend.
Orchestra	To hear one: You will reveal a well-hidden secret.
Order	To receive one: You will get an official position.

Orderly room
To be in one: You will become engaged and will have a happy marriage.

Ordination
To see one: You may have more work to contend with, but the extra cash makes the effort most worthwhile.

Ore
To dig for it: You will uncover a mystery.
To see it: Satisfaction and good luck for you and the members of your family.

Organ
To play one: Your trade will be very beneficial in your future life.
To see one: A family get-together is in the future.

Organist
To hear one playing an organ: You may receive a rather unexpected invitation.

Ornament
To make one: A romance could interfere with your ability to concentrate on your work.

Orphan
To be one: You will experience much trouble and strife throughout your life, but your senior years will be extremely pleasant.

Ostrich
To see one running: It is best to avoid business transactions for the next few days.
To try to catch one: Strangers will cause an unpleasant interruption.

Otters
To feed them: Your life will soon change due to increased social activity.
To see otters is significant of a happy home, a loving companion, and obedient children.

Oven
To place a cake in a heated oven: Don't pay any heed to neighborhood rumors.
To see a roast in an oven: To do the work you love is your choice alone.

Overcoat
To see a nice one: Your luck will return very soon.
To see yourself buying one: Be careful when in an open body of water.
To wear a new one: Honor and dignity.
To borrow one: Uneasiness will remain with you for awhile.

Overflow
Great changes caused by extra money may not be worth the stress.

Oversalt   To taste oversalted food: A family quarrel is in sight.

Overseer   To be one: If you intend to gamble, be sure that it is your money you are risking, and not joint funds.

Overthrow   To suffer one: Don't become excited over something that is absolutely unimportant.

Overture   To hear one: Your expectations will soon be reality.

Owl   To hear one cry out: You will attend a funeral. To see one: Be on the alert; a misfortune is threatening you. To see a stuffed one: Take care of your social security.

Oxen   To see them: Your wishes will be fulfilled and you will become a wealthy and happy person.

Oysters   To buy or to eat them: Keep your spending within reasonable limits.

Oyster shells To dream about oyster shells means that you are probably in an impulsive mood.

Packet   To get one: Strange things will happen during your absence.
                      To send one: You will receive an acceptable proposition.

Pack up   Your belongings: You will take an unexpected journey to a far away place.

Page   To see one: You have a secret love for someone.

Pagoda   To dream of one: You should change your opinion about life.

Pail   To see one: Be satisfied with your job.
                      To see one full of water: You are impatient.
                      To see an empty one: Think seriously about bettering your education.

Pain   If you have pain in your dream: You will have much pleasure and happiness with your children.

Paint   To dream of red paint: If you love, love with all of your heart.
                      To dream about white paint: Trust your sweetheart.
                      To dream about yellow paint: Don't be jealous.
                      To dream of blue paint: Loyalty is the key to your success.
                      To dream of green paint: Be hopeful and optimistic.
                      To dream of black paint: Warns of a separation.
                      To work with paint: Don't mistake your hopes for reality.
                      To see a can full of paint: You may become wealthy through playing the lottery.
                      To paint a house: You will be humiliated.
                      To paint a picture: You will be promoted by a woman.

Paint brush   To work with one: Avoid contact with silly people.

Painting   To buy one: Make amends with people who you may not have seen as often as you would have liked.
                      To sell one: This is a difficult time for the successful handling of money matters.

Palace   To build one: Your arrogance will cause you trouble.

To live in one: There are envious people in your midst.
To own one: Hidden money will cause you trouble.

Pale
To see someone as pale as a ghost: What you agree to now as future policy could cause heavy losses at a later date.
To see yourself pale: Don't challenge people who are in a more advantageous position than you are.

Palette
With paint on it: Favorable times and good luck are ahead of you.

Palisade
To see: Your plans will be interrupted.

Pall bearer
To see one or more of them: An unpredictable time is ahead of you.
To be one yourself: Creative projects must not be allowed to get out of hand.

Palm branch
To see one: You should devote some time to your health.

Palm tree
To see one or more of them: You have comfort.

Pan
To see or to handle one: Your home is your castle. Endeavor to keep it comfortable.

Pancakes
To eat or make them: All of your enterprises will result in success.

Panther
If you should see one in a dream: A well-known personality will take care of you.

Paper mill
If you see or work in one: Your worries about the future are entirely unjustified.

Paprika
Trouble is on the way.

Parachute
See your physician at the first sign of any aches or pains.

Parade
To see one: You have no grounds for complaint; your earnings are good.
Foreign troops: You must take responsibility for your present actions.

Paradise
To see it in your dream: You have a guardian angel.

Paragraph
Your best friends will betray you.

Paralysed

To be: You will be asked to take on new duties. Don't hesitate to take them.

Parasitic insect

To see one: Remember your promise; don't go back on your word.
Commit no sins.
To have insects: No matter how poor you may be right now, in the future you will be wealthy.
To kill one: Your laziness is self-defeating and will cause you trouble.

Parcel

If you see an empty one: You will be the recipient of bad news.
If you send one away: You will have a happy surprise.
If you see a parcel full of money: A creative hobby will hold particular appeal.

Parchment

To see or feel it: Your love life will be lucky.

Pardon

To be pardoned: Realize that not everybody is unsympathetic.

Parents

To see or speak to them: Support from influential people is unlikely to be forthcoming.
If you see your deceased parents in a dream: Very good times are ahead of you.
If you should talk to your dead parents in a dream: Your children will lead successful lives.
To see your parents die: This means that your parents will have very long lives.

Parliament

Unpleasant controversy and discord.

Park

To walk in one: You will live a carefree and happy life.

Parrot

To own one: People will generally praise you.
To teach one: People do not speak well of you.
To see one in a cage: If you treat others with fairness, you will be treated well in return.
To hear one talk: Increase your knowledge of a subject that is of great interest to you.

Parsley

To pick it: You will find a protector.

Partridge

To shoot one: On your journey, it is fine to take along pleasant companions, but it is best to keep your entourage small.
To see one in the forest: Don't count too much on luck alone.

In a meadow: Do not despair - everything will work out well in the end.
Sitting on a roof: Don't lose your patience.
To catch one with your hands: Somebody will cheat you.
To eat one: You will become poor.

Party
To attend one: Good results are best obtained through teamwork.

Passport
To hold one in your hand: You will make a journey to a far away place and you will never return.

Paste
To see or work with: Grief and distress will be with you, but only for a short while.

Pater
To see or talk to: Unpleasant discussions with your employers.

Pastry
To see fresh pastry: Your health will continue to give you cause for concern.
To see old, stale pastry: You will pay the price for a sin committed long ago.
To eat it: Your happiness is short-lived.
To bake it by yourself: Someone will enrage you.

Pasture
A green one: A new approach brings desired results.

Patch
To see one somewhere: Your good life is a direct result of your thriftiness.

Patent
To own one: Someone is trying to trick you or to rip you off. Be cautious and wait for the right time to confront them.
To steal a patent: People laugh about your shortcomings and weaknesses only because they know no better.
If you see someone else stealing a patent: Trust your luck and do not be afraid to put yourself out on a limb today.
If you buy a patent: Foretells of a good profit.

Patent leather
For those of you who are widowed or divorced, a second marriage is a distinct possibility.

Path
To see a very small one: Your proposal will be interrupted.
If you walk on a small path: The punishment you receive will be entirely justified.

Pauper   To see or talk to one: You have no reason to talk of or become excited about the behavior of other people.

Pavement   You will soon reunite with a friend.

Pavillion   Secret love.

Pawnshop   To see or be in one: You are very welcome in somebody's home.
To do business in one: Be cautious - your freedom is at stake.

Pay   To see someone paying for something: You will win something.
If you are paying someone: Take care not to cause yourself any harm.
To be paid: This is a favorable time for team-work with your spouse.

Payday   To dream about: Your worries are unjustified.

Paymaster   To see one: An old debt will be repaid.

Payment   To make one: Now is the time to pay more attention to your diet. If you heed this advice your health and general well being will improve.

Peaches   To eat them: A reunion with your sweetheart.

Peacock   To see one: Be prepared for many days of happiness.
To hear one: Your work will be held in high esteem.

Pearls   To see a string of them: Don't be selfish in discussions of family matters.
To collect them: Be prepared for whatever may happen.

Pears   To preserve them: Be careful - danger lurks just around the corner.
To shake a pear tree: A new and exciting person will enter your life.
To see them hanging on a tree: Good future.
To eat them: You will see somebody you never expected to run into.

Peas   In blossom: All of your ventures will be lucky.
To eat them: You will expand the base of your operation.
To pick them: With due diligence you will reach your goal.

Peat
To see or work with: You wil' money.

Pecans
To eat them: The trouble you a. only temporary and will eventually ... be favorable for you.

Pedal
To see some: You will throw money down the drain.

Peddler
To see or to be one: This is a good omen of profitable business ventures in the near future.

Peep show
To be at or to look at one: You will soon fall deeply in love.

Peewit
To see: Your luck will vanish for the next couple of months.

Peg
To see or work with one: Hindrances will be removed from the path to success.

Penalty
To suffer one: You will be greatly rewarded.
To pay a fine: You must remain cautious about straining yourself.

Pencil
To see or work with one: You will be wrongfully accused of something. Fight back.
To see one on a desk: You will receive good news.

Penitentiary
To see one from the outside: Old worries will once again befall you.
To be an inmate in one: Try to overcome a bad habit.

Pennon
You should not waste your time daydreaming. There are many little things that should be completed.

Pension
To receive one: This is a hint that you should be more concerned about your financial future.

Peony (rose)
If you see one or many of them: You will be successful in love.

People
If you see them on the street or elsewhere: Be extra careful on your next trip or journey.
If you see naked people: You will uncover important secrets.
To see bearded people: You have a reliable business partner.

If you see them imprisoned: You have a rich patron.
If you see many happy people: Foretells of wealth and success.
To see them sleeping: Visitors will make you feel uncomfortable.
If you feel that people are acting strangely towards you: You can count on having a large fortune.
If they appear very intelligent: Don't be overly confident with your situation.

Pepper

To eat it: A problem you had thought was solved will once again require your immediate attention.

Perfume

Misunderstandings with relatives should be discussed and resolved quietly and sensibly.

Perish

In war: An affair of the heart commands more time and attention.

Perjury

To commit it: Warns you of bad luck.

Persecute

Someone: Peace and enjoyment.
To be persecuted: Now is the right time to listen to the advice of older relatives.

Perspiration

Your anxiety is not entirely unfounded.

Perspire

A long distance call requires clarification.

Petition

To sign one: You may experience difficulties at work.

Petroleum

To see or smell it: You make the acquaintance of an interesting individual.

Petticoat

To wear one: Don't be afraid to mix business with pleasure.
To wear a white one: The purchase of a luxury item will contribute to the restoration of peace at home.
To tear one to pieces: You are ignoring something important.

Phantom

To see one: Warns of deception and frightening situations.

Pharmacist

To see or talk to one: You find yourself in unpleasant company.

Pharmacy	To be in one: You fall for usurious trade.
Pheasant	To eat one: Be happy with the company you have. To see one: Now is the time to pay your debts. To shoot one: You never get something for nothing. Beware.
Phonecall	To receive one: This is not the right time to make important financial manoevres, especially speculative ones. To see others using the phone: You will be agitated with people you have not met.
Photograph	Combine your interest in outdoor living and nature with your work and make something profitable out of it.
Photographer	To see one at work: Your own interpretation is the best one.
Phylloxera Vastatric	To see some of them: Your luck is endangered.
Physician	To meet one: Your mate will be supportive of you and you will have good luck and prosperity.
Piano	To hear one: You will be unpleasantly surprised.
Pick up	To pick up a fallen person: You will be called to perform a good deed; therefore, be on the look out for one who may be in need of your assistance. To pick something up from the floor: Unnecessary work.
Pickled herring	To eat: Avoid heavy drinking.
Picklock	To dream about one: Discussing your problems will only lead to arguments right now.
Picture	To see your own: For single people; happy times are ahead. For married people; you and your spouse are back on the right track. If other people show you pictures: You can be certain that you will receive good news. To see a broken one: A bad omen. To see paintings in your dream: Foretells of good business affairs. If you see many paintings, you will be honored.
Picture of a saint	To see this picture in your dream: Don't listen to others; they will only mislead you.

Pies To see a freshly-baked one: Paying attention to diet and nutrition is much more important than you could possibly imagine.
To eat them: You may have to contend with health problems.
To bake one: Be attentive in order that nothing goes wrong in the kitchen.

Pig To see a fat one: Money will come from a surprising source.
If you see many pigs: Unexpected luck will befall you.

Pigeons To eat them: You will insult a friend.
To catch them: You will receive good news from a friend.
To see them fly: This could be your week for power-plays.
To feed them: You will get married soon.
If you see them on a roof: You are getting closer and closer to your goal.
To kill them: A very good friend will move to a far away place.
To see them bill and coo: Don't take any of the things your friends are telling you for granted.

Pike To catch one: Very soon you will find yourself being drawn into social activities.
To see or eat these fish: You will be blessed with old age.

Pilger cane To see or to use one: Take care of your debauchery.

Pilgrim To see one: You will receive a letter from a far away country.

Pilgrimage To see one: You should not fly into a passion.
To attend one: Don't be discouraged; there are many good-hearted people around.

Pill To take one: Calamity.

Pillar To see one: Be good to your children.
If you see a demolished pillar: You should look at people more realistically.

Pillow To see or use one: Somebody will help you to transcend great poverty.
This also means that travel is ill-fated.

If you see a very beautiful one: Your honesty is well known and highly revered.

Pilot

To see or speak to one: You are someone's only hope.

Pins

To see or work with them: You will be struck with an affliction of some sort.

Pincushion

To see one with no pins in it: People praise your enthusiasm.

Pineapple

To see or eat one: Friends or relatives will make an announcement of a forthcoming festive occasion.

Pine marten

To see one or more: You are involved with a tale-bearer.
To see dead ones: Take care of rainy days.

Pipe

If you see a short one: Try to be nice to people. One day you may need them.
If you see a long one: You will progress rapidly.
To smoke one: A very pleasant time is coming up.
To see somebody smoke one: Don't delay important matters. Otherwise, it could be too late to deal with them effectively.
If you see a very expensive pipe: Slow down a bit.

Pirate

Through hard work you will reach your goal.

Pistol

To see one: Try to avoid being angry.
To shoot one: Be aware - danger is just around the corner.

Pit

To dig one: You would have more luck if you weren't so suspicious.

Pitcher

To see one: Good luck is with you.
To break one: This is not the best time for handling important correspondence.

Pitchfork

To carry one: You will remain in your present community for a long time.
To see or work with one: Your livestock will multiply in number.

Place of execution

To see one: Honor and fame.

Plane

To see one: A death will occur among your

friends or acquaintances.
To hear or work on a joiner's bench: A death in your family.

Planks

To see new ones: You may soon move into a new house or apartment.
If they are old and worn: You may have problems with a building, or perhaps you would like to leave your present home.
To buy boards: Two people will reunite.
To cut them: Your ventures will be plagued by troubles.

Plants

To see them in bloom: Lots of happiness in the future.
Dried and dead ones: Beware of sadness and accidents.
Pulling or plucking flowers or greens: You will rid yourself of an undesirable characteristic.

Plate

To break one: Your position is stronger than you originally anticipated.

Platform

To see one with people on it: You are finally coming to grips with problems connected with a close relationship.
To see an empty one: Beware of a dangerous situation.

Playing

To watch somebody: Inheritance.

Playing cards

Clever tricks with: You are in a position to make someone very happy.
To tell one's fortune with: Have faith in your destiny.
To play with: Your expenses must be kept moderate.

Pleasure

To feel: You must continue without hesitation.

Pliers

To see or work with them: Don't be too confident - someone would like to do you harm.

Plot

To hear of or be a member of one: You could put your proposal into effect. If you do, success is a sure thing.

Plough

To see one: By all means, make sure you do nothing which could destroy your home.
To work with one: Good news brings wealth.
To break one: Bad times are ahead of you.

Plums   To pick them: Important new projects should
                   not be started right now. It is best to postpone
                   them for a while.
                   To eat them: You may be able to make some
                   money from something which you have always
                   considered to be nothing but an idle pastime.

Plunder   To see someone plundering. Stubbornness will
                   not make people want to help you.
                   To be involved in one: Concentrate your efforts
                   in the right places. Don't waste your time with
                   unimportant things.

Plush   To see something or to feel something plush:
                   Show people what you can do without their
                   help.

Poacher   To see one: Obey the law. Otherwise, you could
                   end up in jail.

Pocket-knife   If you use one: You will be miserable.

Pocket-watch   To have one: Be discreet and play your own
                   cards.

Poem   To hear or tell one: You will receive a negative
                   answer.

Poet   To see or talk to one: Your own delusions will
                   bring you unhappiness.
                   To be one: In spite of your worries, you main-
                   tain a happy outlook on life.

Pointer   To see one: You gain increased independence.

Poison   To be poisoned: Watch your neighbors. You
                   may have to avoid some of them.
                   To see poison: You will receive no recognition
                   for your help.
                   To take: Great danger and sickness.
                   To see poisonous plants: Sheer spite against you.

Poker   To play it: A loss is caused by a theft.
                   To see somebody playing it: This warns you not
                   to be thoughtless.

Polar bear   To see one: Don't bang your head against the
                   wall.

Pole   To see one: You will be miserable.
                   In the ground: A failure will give you cause to
                   rethink your actions.

Polecat	Don't feel guilty. You acted prudently, therefore you are innocent.
Police	To see one or more of them: Your involvement in a lawsuit will absolve you of suspicion. To talk to them: Your uneasiness is justified. To see them in action: Your trust in somebody will be destroyed.
Politics	Don't forget your familial responsibilities.
Polyp	If you have nasal mucous: You will be forced to take a trip.
Pomegranate	To eat one: Try to participate in surrounding social activities.
Pond	To see one: There will be much happiness in your life. To bathe in one: You can expect to have many children.
Pony	To own or to see one: You will experience happiness and good luck in the near future.
Poodle	If you own one or see one: Your friend is extremely dependable.
Poor	To be poor in a dream: You have peace of mind and good reason to be satisfied with your life. If you see poor people: For lovers; your wishes will come true. For all others; be aware of accidents.
Poorhouse	To see one from the exterior: Bad times ahead of you. If you are an inmate: Be more reserved with strangers.
Pope	To see him in your dream: You are happy and peaceful from the bottom of your heart.
Poplar	You can be happy that your business will soon show improvement.
Poppy head	To see or pick one: A member of your family falls ill.
Poppy seed	To eat: He who lives on hope dies in hunger.
Porcelain	If you are an executive: You have to count on trouble.

If you are from the middle class: You must count on sickness in your family.

Porch
You will be more successful if you don't rely on others.

Porcupine
To see one: Be versatile, but don't spread yourself too thin.

Pork
To see pork meat: You have a faithful spouse.
To eat pork meat: Your luck will likely vanish soon. Let others take the risks for you.

Porpoise
To see one: All of your friends like you, and they have many things to give you.

Porter
To see one: Helpful people will aid you in averting disaster.
To speak to one: Danger of deception increases the need for extra caution and moderation.
To be served by one: Don't miss the next meeting.

Portrait
To see or sit in front of one: Your love life is stable.
To see a portrait of someone who is still alive: The subject of the portrait will live a long life.
To see one of a deceased person: You will receive horrifying news.

Postage stamps
To have, see or buy them: You will make nice new acquaintances.

Poster
If you see one: Surprising news will arrive through the mail.

Postman
To see or speak to one: Your hopes will not be fulfilled if you do not persevere.

Post office
To see one: Someone will try to borrow money from you.
To be in one: Don't spend a small fortune on a gift.

Pot
To see one: You will be spared a dangerous situation.
To break one: Some irritations in the near future.

Potatoes
To eat them: Most of your neighbors like you very much.

To pick them: Part of your hopes become a reality.

Poultry
To see some: One day you will enjoy more than one income.
White: Lady luck is on your side.
Brown: A dangerous situation where an animal is involved.
If you own poultry in your dream: Someone is disloyal to you.
To feed them: Your wealth is increasing.
To kill them: You must rid yourself of intruders.

Powder
To use it: You have done something wrong and are trying to hide it.

Power
To have it: You have caused an unfortunate situation and you should feel lucky that you have come out of it undamaged.
To practise: Don't resign yourself yet.

Prairie
To see: If you relax more often, it will do you some good.

Praise
To give it: Don't trust people who are overly friendly.
To receive it: Your arrogance could destroy a good friendship.
To hear it: Make good use of your energy.

Prayer book
To have one: This is a favorable time for solidifying an old friendship.

Prayers
To listen to a sermon: Do everything in your power to clear the air at home.

Praying
To be: Your undertakings will be fruitful.

Preach
To hear somebody: You will hear sad news.

Prebendary
Your retirement will be carefree.

Pregnant
To be: You will lose a good friend.

Prescription
To get one: You receive false news.

Present
To give one: You will experience a gain.
To receive one: You will experience some loss.

President
To speak to one: You will be disappointed.
To see one: You feel annoyance.

Pressure
To pressure someone: You will be in touch with bad company.

Pretzel	To see one: You have little to worry about as far as your health is concerned. To eat one: You will receive help from all sides.
Pricker	To see or work with: You will be involved in harmful gossip.
Primitive man	To see one: You will hear unbelievable news.
Primrose	To see one: Your efforts will soon be centered on travel preparations.
Prince	To see him: Unpleasant things are happening to your business.
Prison	To see one: Although you did nothing wrong, your conscience still bothers you. To be put into one: Your fears of the future are entirely unjustified.
Prison cell	To see or be in one: You will accomplish more if you will stand on your own two feet.
Printer	To see one at work: You can expect to hear of an inheritance. To see a printing press: You have the opportunity to increase your knowledge or to obtain an honorable job. To observe the printing process: You will receive news from all over.
Printing office	Avoid malicious people.
Procellarians humming-bird	Flying: Your love is endangered. To hear one cry: You will get all the help that you need to succeed.
Procession	To see one: Your conscience won't allow you any peace. To attend one: Peace and happiness at home. To witness one: A quick and successful change will occur.
Profit	To make: Someone is persecuting you for no reason.
Profiteer	To see or talk to one: Your depth of perception leaves a lot to be desired.
Profusion	To have: You will suffer a minor disadvantage within the next few days.

Program	To have one: What appeared to be a solid connection may actually be nebulous. To read one: Your curiosity will get you into trouble.
Project	To have one: A domestic adjustment you made last month will prove to be beneficial.
Promotion	A request for participation in a business matter will be of benefit to you.
Prostitute	To see or talk to one: Learn to say no without creating resentment.
Prostration	You will suffer humiliation at the hands of others.
Protection	To look for: Luck is with you.
Publican Keeper (in England)	A very fine family will invite you to dinner.
Public utility	To see one: Go slowly, study details, be aware of design structure and long-range goals.
Public weighbridge	To see one: Somebody will ask for your opinion about a bizarre matter.
Pudding	To eat some: Tittle-tattle about you.
Puddle	To see one: In the near future, you will experience bad luck.
Puff	To use one: Someone would like to deceive you.
Pulling down	To pull down a scaffold: Acknowledge a bad experience. To demolish a house: You are being deprived.
Pulpit	To see one: Symbolizes pleasure and happiness. To be in one: This is good time for attending to the problems of relatives, especially older ones.
Pump	To see one: This means that you will have a delightful surprise.
Pumpkin	To see one: Relatives who are likely to be difficult can cause you to become impatient and short-tempered.
Pumproom	Postpone making major decisions.
Punch	To drink: Your kindness will be misused by others.

Puppet	To see one: Someone will hinder you in your quest.
Purchase	From time to time, give your spouse a small present.
Purse	To have one: Until now you have had no real reason to be dissatisfied with your life. However, this could change should you become selfish.
Purgatory	To be in: You will have a conflict with the law.
Purple	To see something purple: When you become poor, do not blame others.
Puss	To see it on yourself or on others: Don't make excuses for others; this does not help them in the least. You would help them if instead you would show them how to stand on their own two feet.
Put to sleep	To see somebody put to sleep, or if you do it yourself: Avoid impulsive actions.
Puzzle	To solve one: You will be rewarded with in-gratitude. To be unable to solve one: Although your persistence and skill endear people to you, they have a tendency to take advantage of you.
Pyramid	To see one: You will only achieve happiness when you are far away from home.

Quadrille   To dance one: You attend too many parties.

Quail (bird)   To see one: You are under good protection.
                   To hear one: You may receive bad news.

Quaker   To see one: Differences can be reconciled
                   without losing face.

Quarantine   To be in: Control your passion and then you will
                   be more successful.

Quarrel   To have one: Enemies surround you.
                   To hear other people quarreling: Everyone is the
                   architect of his own fortune.
                   With an acquaintance: Be careful of a street ac-
                   cident.
                   With your spouse: You may feel that a relative
                   has not been entirely honest with you and this
                   could upset your financial plans.

Quarters   You have some bad neighbors - be aware of
                   them.

Quartet   To see or hear one: You will sustain losses.

Quay   To see one: Your lovesickness is groundless.
                   Everything will turn out in your favor.

Queen   To see her: Instinctively, you will make the right
                   decisions.

Questioned   To be: Keep a close eye on your business part-
                   ner.

Quilt   To make or to see one: You will have to give up
                   something if you want to reach your goal.

Quince   To eat: Several jealous people are around you.

Quoit   To play: Avoid money speculation.

Rabbi   To talk to one: Success in business.

Rabbit   To see one run: In the very near future you will have to make a decision quickly.
To see rabbits in a cage: Something unexpected will frighten you.
To eat a roast hare: You will find yourself enjoying life more in the future.

Raccoon   To see one: If you are sick, don't postpone seeing a doctor.
To feed them: Means good health and a long life.
To kill one: You must overcome a setback.

Race   To see one: Your dissatisfaction on your job is based in your inadequacy. Study it more closely and it will give you more confidence in yourself.
To be in one: You will encounter some barriers on the way to success.

Race course   Check behind the scenes and you will be surprised.

Racket   To play with one: Don't get involved in adventures over which you don't have strict control.

Rack railway   To see or ride on one: Think twice before starting a new venture.

Rack wagon   To see one: Do not lose confidence in yourself.
To drive one: Time is on your side, so you can afford to play a waiting game.

Radio   To see one: Stay with the projects you have started.
To hear one: Pleasure and business should be two different things. You can seldom combine them successfully.

Radish   To eat one: You know how to save money - why don't you do it?
To prepare: Don't jump to conclusions.

Raffle   To see one: Go easy with your personal spending.

Raft   To see one: You will have success in your new business.

Raft timber   To see it in the water: You will receive help at the right time.

Rafters

To see one built: You will be wrongfully accused by a family member.
To see a new one: Means long life if you remain with your present lifestyle.
To see an old one: You cannot be too careful where cash is concerned.

Rage

To be in one: An unavoidable lie is still a lie. Think about it.

Ragout stew

To eat it: Don't throw your money away: you will need it.

Rags

To see: Money is not a problem in your life.

Raid

If you see one: You will be persuaded to do something.
If you are the victim of one: You will discern that your first idea is the best.

Railway

To see one: A member of the opposite sex could make a scene.
To take a journey by railway: Avoid a dispute with the IRS (International Revenue Service).
If you see railway freight cars: An unexpected visitor will arrive.
If you are in one: A present involvement will proceed rapidly.

Railway official

To see or speak with one: A journey is in sight, but it can also mean unpleasant news is ahead.

Rain

With sunshine: Success is around the corner.
If you see any rain: Your performance is marvelous and you will be rewarded.
To get wet: Loss of a dear person.
If you see very heavy rain in a dream: Disaster may threaten you.

Rainbow

To see one: Someone is playing games with your love.

Raisins

To see or work with them: Dispute with your neighbors.
To eat raisins in a dream: You may have to change your job and homestead.

Rake

To see or work with one: Your precise attitude will make you many enemies.

Ram

To see one: Arguments over an inheritance could break out.

Rape

To be endangered by one: You may be impeded by an illness.

To be a victim of: Be very careful about getting involved in any affairs that could result in a lawsuit.

Rasp

To see or work with: The coming month will be a difficult one.

Raspberries

To see or eat them: Look for new ways to increase you earnings.

Rash

To see yourself with pimples all over: It means much wealth for the dreamer.

Rats

To see them: Friends will cheat you.
To catch them: You will stop a theft.

Rattle

To see or hear one: You will receive an unexpected letter that will surprise you.

Raven

To hear one cry: You experience loss and damage.
To see one: Misery in your stable.
To see one on a tree: Death in your neighborhood.

Raw meat

To eat it: Foretells of displeasure.

Razor

To handle one: Is a warning to be cautious of a dangerous undertaking. It also warns you of gossip.

Read

Handwriting: You will succeed in mostly everything.
Printed matter: You only acquire opulence through work.
A book: The time has not yet come for you.

Reaper

To see one at work: Do everything to get things straightened out.

Rebellion

Study a message for a valuable hint.

Receipt

To get one: You will make a new friend.
To write one: Take care of your enemies.

Receptionist

To talk to one: The irritation you suffer from is your own fault.

Recipe

This is a good period for work if you are engaged in research.

Reconcile	Make one's peace: A family dispute is very possible.
Reconciliation	With somebody: Your effort will be successful.
Recruit	Your wages are too little for the hard work you are doing.
Rectory	To see or be in one: Your sweetheart will leave you behind.
Red currant	To eat: This will be a happy time for romance.
Red pencil	To have one: Take care of your money.
Reed	To cut one: You will lead a peaceful life.
Reef	To see: Surprising events can cause serious upsets.
Referee	To see one in action: Your social life will improve soon.
Refinery	Don't be greedy - it won't bring you any profit.
Refreshment	To receive refreshment: With your own power you will take yourself to the top. Refusing refreshment: You have a powerful will, but you are not businesslike. Give it to someone else: Don't wait for something in return if you give something away. To have: You get what you want, but not in the manner you originally anticipated.
Regatta	To see one: Your vanity gets you into trouble.
Registered letter	To receive one: Don't fear a test - you will be successful.
Regret	To have a feeling of regret in your dream: Foretells unpleasantness. Someone is showing regret towards you: Foretells of luck.
Reindeer	To see one: Do not try to force people to agree with your ideas.
Rejoicing	To hear: Unforeseen events may upset your plan.
Relatives	To see or speak to them: You are a battler for justice. Many find you have an abrasive personality.

To see them die: Unpleasantness with your neighbors.

Relieve nature   To do: Mind your reputation.

Relic   You are distressed.

Relief   Your know how is misunderstood by others.

Rent   If you rent an apartment in a dream: Circumstances are deteriorating.

Report   To do: Unnecessary spending.

Reprieve   To be: Apprehension and gossip.

Reprimand   If you believe that you have scolded someone in your dream, you may experience trouble. You may avoid it if you reconsider the circumstances and your leniency.

Reptile   If you see one in your dream: Don't be afraid. All through your life you will meet good people.

Request   To refuse a request: A lost item will be found again.
You ask a request: You will experience humiliation.
If you see or receive a begging letter: Never give your spouse a reason to think you have betrayed him/her or done something wrong.

Requisition   To sue for debt: You may profit by gambling.

Rescue   Somebody: You may have to act on behalf of an older relative. This could be connected in some way with the transfer of property from one person's name to another, or perhaps a will.
To be rescued: You will be honored in your old age.

Resentment   To feel: You will be overloaded with work in the near future.

Residence   To see one: You sure have good luck with the opposite sex.

Respect   To render it to other people: Somebody will humiliate you.
To receive it: You will be involved in a court case.

Restaurant   To be in one: If someone wants to talk to you, don't disappoint them.

Resting	To be in a dream: You will have difficulties concentrating.
Restrain	If you do: You have a messy budget. Try to bring it into order.
Retailer	To see or be one: You have plenty of everything. Share your fortune with your relatives.
Revenge	To take: You are going through a tough time in your personal life.
Revival	To attend a religious one: Don't complain about your family life. The trouble you are having right now is your own fault.
Revolver	To have one: You could triumph over your enemies, but you are too slow.
Revue	To see one in your dream: A restriction will be transformed into an opportunity.
Rheumatism	To feel it in a dream: You have somebody around you that you can't get rid of.
Rhinestones	To see or wear them: Express your individuality in dealing with people around you.
Rhinoceros	If you see or touch one: Foretells of good luck.
Rhododendron	If you see one in blossom: A lost cause will reverse itself.
Rhubarb	To eat or to prepare it: After a misfortune you find luck and happiness.
Rib	To see your own or to break them: Nevertheless, people will be thankful to you. To eat ribs: Differences at home will escalate.
Ribbon	To see colorful ones or to decorate yourself with them: You are conceited and because of this people don't tell you the whole truth.
Rice	To eat it: Means health and a long life. To cook it: You are on the road to recovery.
Riddles	To solve them: If you want to achieve anything you will have to settle for compromised solutions.
Riding school	To attend one: You have a good chance of putting yourself in line for a promotion in the near future.

Rifle

To see or handle one: Your concepts are original, often controversial, and you are creative, inventive, sensual and stubborn.

Ring (on your hand)

To see one: Be receptive to a request from one who is temporarily disabled.
To wear one: You can expect more than one child.
To lose one: Someone will insult you.
To find one: Disagreements with your business partner.
Made of brass: Your future is full of anxiety.
Made of gold: Marriage blessings.
A broken one: Means disturbance.

Ring (of a bell)

To hear a bell ring: News will irritate you.
To ring a bell by yourself: Sometimes you have to use elbow grease.

Ring circle

To put a rim on a barrel: You make new connections.

Riot

To be in one: Means quarrels and fights with your best friends.

Rise

Getting out of bed: You are too excited about your plans. Maybe you should think them over again.
If a sick person dreams of getting out of bed: In the near future you will feel better.

Rival

To have one: People will accuse you of things you really have done but that you never thought they would find out.

River

To see one with clear water: Have more pride in yourself.
To see a wild one: Stick to normal ways to earn money.
To see a river flooded: Work as long as you can. Don't think of your retirement yet.
To see a very bright river: Health problems will not interfere with your work.
To bathe in a river: Don't be careless with money - you will need it at a later date.
To fall into one: Gambling is unlikely to pay off.

Rivet

To see or work with one: Don't be a spendthrift.

Roadway

To see or to use one: Pay attention to matters before it is too late.

Roaring storm	To witness one: Someone will play a dirty trick on you.
Roast	To prepare or to see one prepared: Quarrels with your brother or sister.
Rob	To be robbed: You will lose some of your closest friends.
Robe	To see or to wear one: A happy family get-together in the very near future.
Robber	To see one or more: Somebody will threaten you. To be attacked by one: Big inheritance.
Robin	To see and hear this bird in a dream: You have the full confidence of your co-workers. Do not disappoint them.
Rocket	To see one: Making extra money through a side occupation might be worth investigating a little further. To hear one take off: The road to success will be a hard one for you.
Rock garden	If you see one, work or walk in one: Do not dig your heels in too much. You could hurt the one you love.
Rocking chair	To see one or to sit in one: This is not the time to take a loan or to take on new commitments.
Rocks	To see or walk on them: Discord with friends or loved ones.
Rogue	To dream about one: Through caution you prevent a felony from being done to you.
Roll call	To see: Before leaving home, make sure that all safety precautions have been taken.
Roller-skate	Don't live quite so much within your memories.
Roof	With shingles: In the very near future you will receive a pleasant message. Without shingles: Be aware of a disaster close to your home. With red shingles: Means satisfaction and happiness. To see a roof on fire: The power of your soul will not fade.

With birds on it: Those who appear to be quiet may actually be hiding their emotions.

Roofer   To see one at work: Straighten out your budget.

Roof tiles   To see or work with them: Basic material should be reviewed, as you will be asked questions about it.

Room   To have: Somebody will quit on you.
To have a bright one: You will be promoted very soon.

Rooks   To see this bird in a dream: There is a danger of accidents if you allow your mind to wander when on the job.

Rooster   Fighting: Your cruelty from time to time will backfire.

Root   From a tree: Reserve time for romance.
To fall over one: If you want to succeed you will have to be business-like.
To see one of a tooth: Your sickness is not dangerous.

Rope   To see or to handle one: A family discussion will not be fruitful.
To buy it: Bad times ahead of you. Don't lose your temper.

Rosary   See in prayer: Death in your family.
To have: Sickness in your home; don't delay calling a doctor.

Roses   To see roses: Means respect.
A yellow one: Loss.
A red one: Friendship.
A white one: You receive a present.

Rose bush   A party with all the family members is in sight perhaps a wedding is coming up.

Rosemary   If you pick it in a dream: Foretells of good profit in your business.

Rower   Yourself: Plan your travel arrangements very carefully.
To see somebody row: Barriers come tumbling down. You must take definite strides into the future.

Rubber   To see or to handle it: Some of your friends'
                     words are not very reliable.

Rudder   To see or handle one: You will be successful if
                     you set out on a search.

Rude   If you see yourself being rude: Don't be scared
                     of enemies, because you don't have any.

Ruin   To be in one or to see a ruin from the outside:
                     Take care of your future because nobody will
                     give you financial help in your old age.

Rum   To drink it: Friends will announce their visit.
                     To see it in a bottle: Stay where you are - don't
                     follow any foolish advice.
                     To smell it: Don't try to get secrets out of other
                     people. It may cause you harm.
                     To spill it: Much that you are told is private and
                     you are trusted with confidential material.

Rumbling noise   To hear it in a dream: Be extra careful when
                     driving; there is a danger of an accident due to
                     negligence.

Runic inscription To try to read one: Your secret will not be
                     discovered.

Running   If you see yourself running in a dream: It would
                     be unpardonable if you didn't work on your
                     enterprise. You will give away your success.

Rush   To see someone: Deceptive hopes.

Rust   To see somewhere: Feel free to ask your children
                     to do something for you.
                     If you see rust spots in linen: It is a waste of time
                     to wait for a visitor who promised you his com-
                     pany.
                     On metal: You should not trust everybody.
                     On a knife: Take a closer look at your col-
                     leagues.

Rye   To eat rye or to see it: This dream is an omen of
                     good luck.

Rye bread   To eat it: Don't be tempted into giving up your
                     responsibility to other people.

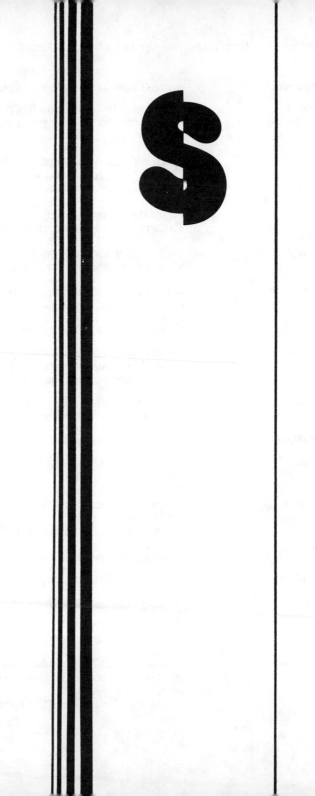

Sabbath   A careless mistake could ruin your reputation.

Sabre   To see one: Just when you feel that you need help the most is the time you are least likely to get it.

Sacks   Filled with grain: A member of the opposite sex does care, and may prove it to you.
Filled with fruit: Your prestige rises to a higher level.
To see them empty: Grief.
To carry them: Honor and wealth.

Sacred   To be sacred: Get your point across, no matter what the circumstances may be.

Sacrifice   It will be difficult to gauge exactly what is going on in your boss' mind.

Sacristy   To see one: You will be invited to a christening.

Saddle   To slip out of one: Luck with gambling.
To see one: Your business slacks off.
To sit in one: You will make money easily.

Safe   To see one: Think twice before you spend too much money on entertainment.

Saffron   To eat it: A friend will die.

Sage   To prepare it: A long and healthy life is ahead of you.

Sail   To see one inflated: In spite of everything, luck is with you.
To see a ragged one: Take care of your luck or it will fade.
To repair one: Affliction will befall you.

Sailors   To see them: Your journey will be dangerous.

Salad   To eat it: You may look forward to a promotion.

Salami   To see it: Very little satisfies you.

Salary   To receive one: There could be some errors in bills that you receive. It is best to check them over.
To pay one: You will win the fight.

Saliva	To see it: Frauds and quarrels are of your own doing. To have it on you: Unbelievable luck.
Salmon	To catch one: A romantic experience lies ahead. To eat one: You will gradually become accustomed to your new surroundings.
Salt	To eat some: A wish will come true. To spill some: Troubles at home. To see salt: It is a healthy sign that you regret your violent actions.
Saltwater	To drink it: Pardon people who were rude to you.
Salute	To an acquaintance: With proper treatment, a minor health problem you have had recently should clear up. To an enemy: Don't heed the rumors of strangers.
Sample	To see them: Influential people will exhibit great understanding of your efforts.
Sand	To spread it out: Focus your attentions on relatives who may call or visit without notice.
Sand pit	To see one: Don't put yourself into an embarrassing situation.
Sardelles	To eat them: Don't be impatient with family members.
Sardines	To buy them: If you follow the right path, you will be successful.
Sash	To wear one: This is an excellent time to study for an examination.
Satan	Nothing but quarrels will erupt if you adopt a heavy-handed approach.
Saturday	Minor disappointments will disrupt your daily routine.
Sausages	To buy them: Your investment will grow. To eat them: Your next big purchase will be a bargain. To make sausages: You may be offered a job in another city or perhaps abroad. To fry them: This is an exceptionally good time

for those who have the opportunity to devote more time and attention to their home lives.

Saw	To work with one: Somebody will humiliate you.
Sawdust	Recovery from your illness.
Sawmill	There may be a slowdown at your place of employment, which may be caused by an industrial dispute.
Scab	To have one on your head: Parents will encounter difficulties in dealing with the problems of their children.
Scaffold	To see one being erected: You may soon have an occupation with several dangerous side effects. Apart from these dangers, this occupation promises you great advantage and prosperity. If you climb on one: Continue to do everything in your power to save more and more money. To descend one: You should postpone important business transactions for the time being.
Scale	To see one: Your good luck is hanging by a thread. Be careful in your conversations with other people.
Scandal	With your husband: Settle a dispute with a loved one before it is blown all out of proportion. With your wife: Seize an unusual opportunity before it slips out of your grasp. With neighbors: Any attempt to increase your knowledge of a specific subject will be rewarding. To hear one: Dispute with your best friend.
Scar	To have one: You will reach an old age, and will have carefree senior years. To see one on somebody: Don't try to communicate with poorly-educated people.
Scarecrow	To see one: You may expect terrifying news.
Scared	To be: You become involved in a dangerous situation and are unable to escape from it.
Scarf	To wear one: You will be honored at a special occasion. To buy one: Try and cash in on the good fortune surrounding you.

Scarlet fever You will make an important contact which could signify the start of something big.

Scavenger To see one: You discover loopholes, become aware of basic procedures and are therefore better able to rebuild a more solid base.

Scenery You may receive an invitation, but be careful, for people will try to interrogate you.

Scholar To be one: Any plans related to domestic issues that you are thinking of putting into operation will receive total support.
To see several scholars: You will receive great recognition from your peers.

School To attend one: Your future is stable.
To teach in one: Don't become excited over minor things, as they are bound to happen anyway.

Schoolmaster To talk to him: Influential people will encourage you to implement new methods.

School report To read one: You should think of your own past before you judge the actions of others.

Scissors To buy a pair of: Your life is economically viable. Don't make any changes right now.
To sharpen them: Quarrels at home are indicated.

Scissors grinder To see one: Foretells pleasant, exotic overseas travel.

Scold Someone will try to expel you.

Scorpion To see one: With regard to your career aspirations, it would be beneficial if you would rid yourself of false illusions.

Scotch pine To see several of them: If you live in moderation, you will have a long life.
To collect pine cones: Loved ones will show great sympathy and understanding for all that you have been through.

Scraper To work with one: You have good friends and true love.

Scratch Yourself: Don't be party to neighborhood rumors.

Somebody else: This is not the right time to contemplate changing jobs.

Scream To hear someone: Social gatherings present the possibility of bringing you into contact with people who are able to give your career a boost.
If you hear yourself screaming: Many differences could arise for those of you who a married.

Screech owls To hear them cry: There is nothing you can do to avoid an unfortunate incident.
To see them: Beware of an accident - disaster is in the air.

Screws To find them: You will be the center of attention at the next party.
To buy them: Don't become involved with unpleasant things.
To work with them: There is no need to hurry; you have plenty of time to complete your projects.

Script You will lose something of value.

Scrub You will find a job which you do not like.

Scull An emotional burden is lifted from your shoulders.

Sculptor To see one at work: You will shine and make a good impression.

Scythe To see a broken one: Take good care of your children.
To work with one: Pay attention to the dangers of road traffic.

Seagulls To see them fly: You are losing confidence in your surroundings.

Seal To seal a letter: Hurry with your proposition.
To have one: You will be honored.

Seaport To be in one: Have caution - there are some bad times ahead.

Search light To see one: You feel a sense of purpose and determination after a period of restlessness.

Sea wall To see one: A friend will play an important role in your life.

Second (in duels)	To be: If you listen, you will learn a great deal.
Secret	If you hear of one: Good friends are not quite as honest as they would have you think. To give a secret away: Your honor is endangered by gossip.
Seeds	To buy them: Your proposal shows signs of progress.
Seeds man	You will conduct business with exorbitant people.
Sell	Something: Don't sell valuable things for less than their true worth. It is best to wait until the price is right.
Semolina	To cook or eat it: You will find that things are slowing down considerably.
Senator	To see one: Someone will ease your embarrassment.
Serenade	To listen to one: Warns of untrue friends or lovers. This also warns of disillusioned hopes and wishes. To be involved with playing one: Good expectations and promises of success in money market dealings.
Sermon	To write one: Employment is likely to take quite a lot out of you. To read one: Don't be a fool; stay exactly as you are.
Serpent	To see one in your dream indicates: You should try to reach an agreement with your mate or partner which would provide you with ways to cut down on unnecessary expenditures.
Servants	To see them at work: Don't make any binding agreements. If you envision yourself as one: It may be a good idea to plan ways in which you might spend your next vacation. To see them arguing in the house: Some difficulties may arise within your household.
Setter	To have one: You will have no difficulty concentrating on endeavors which employ your natural skills and talents.

Seven	To see this number in your dream means: Special relationship, exciting changes, and romance.
Sewing	To do: You will be cleared of suspicion. To start and never finish: A lover is waiting for you. To be hurt while sewing: Unwelcome people will visit your home.
Sewing machine	To dream of one: An affair will soon end.
Sewing things	To work with: Do not talk about other people.
Sexual intercourse	To have: Don't try to buy the affection of one with whom you would like to have a permanent relationship. To see sex organs: Follow your instincts and trust your own judgment. It will be difficult to gauge whether or not your spouse is being totally honest with you.
Shackles	To see them: Sickness may occur
Shadow	To see your own: This is a good time to deal with official matters.
Shaft	To touch one: You must work very hard to overcome poverty. To see a broken one: Think carefully before making any investment where there could be an element of risk.
Shake out	To shake out a table cloth: Your heart will be freed from grievous and unpleasant people. To shake out a blanket: In a short while you will reach your goal.
Shame	To witness: You will receive a beautiful gift.
Shameless	To be: Someone will inquire about your past.
Shamrock	To plant one: You should take more time for rest and relaxation, rather than for the furthering of your business aims. To eat one: A sick relative will soon recuperate. To see a field of shamrocks: Your next business trip will be successful.
Shark	To see one: You will be disturbed by people with a tendency to exaggerate.

To see a dead one: A personal plan may be speeded up if you keep spending to a minimum.

Sharpen   An axe: It would be wise to ascertain the limits of your rights and permissions.

Shaving   To see yourself: Be cautious of fraud and falsity.

Sheaves   To bind them: Your work will be well rewarded. To see them in a field: This is not a good time for romance.

Shawl   To wear one: If you are sick, follow the advice of your physician.

Shed   To see an old one: Don't give up hope; a pile of money is on the way.

Sheep   To see them in a pasture: Be cautious if you are planning to take a trip.
To kill them: Don't be too trusting when dealing with comparative strangers.
To tend them: Don't shirk duties that are better dealt with now than later.

Sheep's wool   To spin it: Take care of your possessions.
To clean it: Your efforts will soon be rewarded.

Sheet   To put one on your bed: Do all you can to improve your mind.
To dream of a sheet of paper: You will receive a letter or other news.
Also, you will be prosperous in your work.

Sheet metal   To buy, trade, or work with it: Don't get bogged down by lengthy discussions which you have little hope of winning.

Shells   To work with: You must take over a serious responsibility.
To buy them: A family annoyance.
To see them on shore: Watch your temper and avoid impulsive actions.

Shelter   If you see yourself building one: You are uncomfortable in your present surroundings.
If you are seeking shelter: Don't expect too much in the near future.

Shepherd   To talk to one: A good opportunity for a business transaction presents itself.
To see a shepherd with a herd: For the time

being, you will have to shelve changes that you wished to make to future policies.
To be one: Don't neglect familial responsibilities.

Sheriff

To dream about a sheriff: Judgment and intuition hit target.
Focus on production, promotion, money and love.

Shield

To see one: You have a good friend and supporter.

Ship

On the water: You are flamboyant with luck.
To see one under water: Be on the alert; danger could threaten your security.
To ride on one: You can count on success.
To navigate one: Be ambitious about reaching your goal.
To see one without a mast: Good times are ahead for you.
To see one sink: Happy tidings in the near future.
To see one burning: Because the law is on your side, you will be the victor.
To see one arriving at port: Don't be jealous of a helpful friend.
To anchor a ship: Your softness is a barrier to your success.
To see people disembarking from one: You will receive an invitation.
To see one shipwrecked: Select your friends more carefully.
To see one on the ocean: Trust in God.
To see one on the shore: Plan your next vacation with great care.
To see one being built: Uncertainty in love.
If you see yourself leave a ship: You will survive a great danger.

Shirt

To dream of putting on a clean shirt: The help you receive from others makes your life more comfortable.
To wear a dirty one: You will probably work better if you are on your own.
To see shirts being washed and ironed: Watch out for deception. No one is as honest and straight forward as you would wish.

Shoemaker	To see him at work: Take it easy with your work.
Shoes	To see wooden ones: You will lose some of your customers.
	To try some on: Take care to ensure that your feet remain healthy.
	To wear new ones: Be creative and try new ideas.
	To see old ones: A friend will cause you much trouble.
	To wear brown ones: Everything will turn out in your favor.
	To see black ones: Don't believe in everybody; someone may try to betray you.
	To collect shoes: Think of others also; they may need your help.
	To buy them: You will be involved in a lawsuit.
Shoot	To see someone shooting: You have to depend on your friends.
	To do it yourself: You must take time to attend to the desires of loved ones.
Shore	To be on one: Don't waste your money.
Shorthand	To write: You will complete a project successfully.
Shotgun	To buy one: Money is not always the solution to your children's problems.
Shot wound	To receive one: Your friends will criticize your behavior in public.
Shoulders	To see broad ones means: Strength and happiness.
	To see them hunched: Your application will be denied.
Shout	To hear somebody: Watch your enemies.
	To hear yourself: You may obtain greater freedom of action.
Shovel	To work with one: A member of the opposite sex is looking for a commitment from you.
Show-case	To look into one: Don't be tempted to eat in expensive restaurants, as they are far beyond your means.
Shower bath	To dream about one: Cooperative efforts lay the groundwork for good luck.

Shrubbery	To see it: You will be happy with your love. To hide behind some: This is a good time for handling the business side of a game or league.
Shrapnel	You may have need to confer with an attorney.
Shriek	If you scream out a message in your dream: You may have to cut down on unnecessary expenditures.
Sick	To be: Health problems could slow you down and force you to rearrange your lifestyle.
Sickbed	To see one: There is no point dwelling on unhappy memories.
Sick person	To see one deceased: All at once you will find a way of becoming rich.
Sickle	To work with one: Your popularity will increase.
Sigh	Poverty and grief won't go away.
Signal flash	Although your hopes have misled you, there is still enough time to start over.
Signalman	To see him at work: Continue to be careful when handling dangerous equipment. There is always a danger of accidents through negligence.
Signet ring	To see one: You can rely on the discretion of your friend.
Silk	To buy it: You will hurt yourself. To see it: A very good outlook for the next few days.
Silk dress	To buy one: Differences with a partner may develop over money.
Silk hat	To see one: Unless you cease your chatter, you will become the laughing stock.
Silk mill	You will make new friends at the next party you attend.
Silkworm	Nothing will go well for you at this time. Try not to be too adventurous.
Silly	To be: Your happiness will be interrupted by ill-tempered and jealous friends.
Silo	To see a full one: Good luck and blessings. To see an empty one: Your bad luck is your own fault.

Silver	To see a silver bowl: Today, you will probably be happier with your own company than with that of the whole gang. To see a large piece of silver: Good times are not on your side.
Singing	To hear children: Contact an influential person who has been of help to you in the past. To hear old people sing: Dissociation from family members. To hear nuns singing: Fortune favors you now, so you can afford to be bold. To hear monks singing: Extravagant spending on yourself and your creative projects is not wise at this time. To hear a chorus: Don't impulsively lose your temper. If you do, you could lose your job. To sing in a basement: Dark clouds appear - you may be in for a romantic disappointment. To sing in the open: Use all of your charms to achieve the appropriate ends. To sing a child to sleep: Your family will support you through an unpleasant time. To hear yourself sing out of tune: You have good reason to be happy.
Single	To be: You will be asked to assume additional responsibilities at work.
Siskin	To hear one: Be discreet when dealing with that special person in your life. To see one in a cage: Luck is with you.
Sister	To dream about her: You will make a very good business connection.
Sister-in-law	To see her: A happy surprise awaits you.
Sit	On a chair: If possible, take a vacation. On something: You will meet a nice man or woman.
Skates	To see them: There is some trouble at home with your children.
Skating rink	To skate on one: Your luck is not yet certain.
Skein	To see one: People will not take a very sympathetic view of your present difficulties.
Skeleton	To see one: Meditation will help you to find an important answer.

Skeleton key	To have one: Don't give in to temptation.
Sketch	A change of residence is almost a sure thing.
Ski	Cross-country: Personal responsibilities multiply. Downhill: Permit others to express their views.
Ski jump	To see one: Don't be so dubious.
Skin	To have marks on your skin: If you need advice of a personal nature, your relatives could prove to be helpful. To have sunburned skin: You will be accused of wrongdoings.
Skipper	To see one: All of your wishes will come true within the next short while.
Skirt	A light-colored one: Despise those who are trying to get you into trouble. A dark-colored one: You will be promoted to a better position.
Skull	To see one: Someone is trying to give you some advice.
Sky	To dream of a blue sky: Avoid risks; adhere to the usual ways of making money. To see a cloudy sky: A romance will be rather unhappy and will probably end soon. To see the evening sky turning red means: Enemies will overtake and defeat you in rivalry.
Skyscraper	To see one: Don't waste time - start saving money now.
Slander	Nobody has asked you for your opinion. It will be best if you will keep quiet.
Slap	To receive one: A long and happy marriage. To give one: Someone will mislead you - be on the lookout.
Slate	To see: You will win a prize in the lottery.
Slater	To see one on a roof: You will be able to do pretty much as you like, which should suit you just fine.
Slaughter	To slaughter an animal: A contract signed now would make the future more secure.

Slaughterhouse   To be in one: If you would lose some weight, your health would improve.

Slaves   To dream about them: Look after your dignity.

Sledging   Your business is stagnating. You may require outside professional advice.

Sleep   To see yourself sleeping: A short trip could prove to be useful for contacting people to whom you wish to talk.
To sleep in church: Pay no heed to news which is not confirmed.
To see others sleep: Watch your alcohol consumption.
Sleep-walking: Contempt is your punishment.

Sleeve   If you wear a long-sleeved dress in your dream: In order to make your life easier, you must have more confidence in yourself and in your friends.
To cut sleeves from a pattern: If you will apply a steady effort to routine chores, you will at least accomplish something.

Slide   To see one: Be prepared for a variety of different sensations.
To slide down one: Good news will make you very happy.

Sling   To make one: You won't end up with the boy or girl you're in love with right now.

Slippers   To get a new pair of them: You will sacrifice something for a friend.
To wear them on the street: You are dissatisfied with your married life.

Slope   To see a stone-covered one: You will have to take some care to avoid overindulgence.
To see one overgrown with moss: You may have the opportunity to push a lucrative business deal through at rapid speed.
To see a wooded slope: You may receive a letter which will help you to decide about the best way of dealing with your creative venture.

Smallpox   To see yourself covered with them: You have found that you are on the wrong track. Take time out to rethink your actions.

Smell   To smell a pleasant eau de cologne: You may be

able to reach a favorable agreement with your partner.
To smell the bad odor of a skunk: If is important and beneficial for you to communicate with your relatives.

Smoke

To see it coming out of a chimney: Luck and peace at home.
To see black smoke: Disillusionment and annoyance.
To see the smoke of a cigarette: Your luck is changeable.

Smoking

To see someone smoking a cigar: Your destiny will follow a constant path.

Snails

To eat them: You will escape a dangerous situation.

Snakes

To see them in a cage: Be aware - there is a chance that one of your children will cheat you.
To see small ones: Don't lose your temper if somebody tries to insult you.
To kill one: Your rude behavior will not be admired by others.
If they bite you: You may feel a sense of discomfort for a short while.

Snare

To see one: Avoid holding onto the past for purely sentimental reasons.

Sneeze

If you see yourself sneezing: Permanent good health for you.

Snouts

To see them: Your own faults will cause you inconvenience.

Snow

To be rubbed with it: Your own stupidity may cause you to suffer a loss.
To see clean, white snow: You worry yourself unnecessarily.
To see dirty snow: You must alter your proposal.
To be in a snowstorm: Unpredictable associates may be unable to live up to promises that they verbally made.
If you see snowflakes falling: You now have the capability of discerning long range possibilities.

Snow geese

To see them flying: The letter you await will arrive soon.

Soap	To wash yourself with soap: An approach will bring the desired results.
Soap bubbles	To see them: Think twice before starting something new.
Sob	If you sob in your dream: After much bad luck, you will become successful.
Soccer	To see this game: Be sure that you make the best of the present opportunities.
Socks	To put them on: Think before you speak. To knit them: You will discover the reason that something has been kept a secret.
Soda water	To drink it: Keep an eye on your money.
Sofa	To rest on one: Unless you are the leader, you will not achieve success. To see a very nice one: God helps those who help themselves.
Soil	To cultivate it: Your friends are very reliable. To see dark, rich soil: A profitable time will go faster than you expect. To plant some seeds in: Your yearning will soon be fulfilled.
Solar eclipse	If you are planning ahead for a long range project, people will have confidence in your abilities.
Soles	To see them: Don't delay outstanding matters.
Son	To see him: Familiar situations will be viewed in a new light. To talk to him: You will receive a letter containing important, notable information.
Son-in-law	To visit him: You will become aware that you are supporting the wrong side.
Song	To sing one: Watch your health. You may need a physical check-up.
Sooty	To be: Luck and winning will change your entire life.
Sore	To have one: Realize that your involvement is serious.
Sorcerer	To see one: Pleasure will follow apprehension.

Sound
To hear: Don't regret any money you spend on things which bring you a lot of enjoyment.

Soup
To prepare it: You will be involved in a bad dispute.
To cook one: Routine affairs may contain problems with your next of kin.
To eat it: Now is the time to have a happy romance.

Soup bowl
To fill one up: What begins as a routine task could become an interesting challenge.

Sowing
To see somebody: You are forced to make a trip.
To do it yourself: A close friend will bring you wealth.

Spark
To see a shower of sparks: It is time for your power play.

Sparrows
To see them: All you get from your boss are empty promises.
To see many of them: Don't be a party to bad gossip.
To hear them: You may become involved in an unpleasant affair.

Sparrow-hawk
To see one: Somebody will steal from you.

Spasm
To have one: As much time as possible should be allotted for rest and relaxation.

Speak
To be willing but unable to speak: You will not agree with your partner's decision, but you would be best to go along with it in order to avoid quarrelsome situations.

Spear
To throw one: Consultation with a professional will dispel any lingering fears that you had over a minor ailment.

Spelling
To teach it to children: You may use an unfair advantage to attain success in your endeavor.
To learn it: Someone with considerable power may offer you valuable hints.

Spelling book
To read one: A major wish will soon be fulfilled.

Spica
To see them: Don't borrow money - it is hard to repay it.
To pick them up from the ground: Don't start something you have no intention of finishing.

Spices	To dry them: People with no conscience may talk about your secret. To buy some: You may have problems with a friend who holds you in confidence.
Spider	To see a large one: It would be in your best interest to make certain concessions. To kill one: Your anger may cause you to have a period of inconvenience.
Spider web	To see a spider spinning a web: Your work brings you happiness. To destroy one: A major change occurs on the homefront.
Spikes	To see them: You can do a lot to repair damage that has been done to a close personal relationship.
Spindle	To see one: A short trip will involve a cousin.
Spinning wheel	To dream about one: You will receive an unusual social invitation.
Spitting	If you spit at someone: The advice of friends should be used cautiously.
Splinter	To remove one from your finger: Don't be arrogant - it will give people a negative opinion of you.
Split	Of a container: A disaster may threaten you.
Spoil	Children: Ingratitude is certain. Somebody: You may profit in a lottery.
Sponge	To see one: Greediness is not a desirable trait; try to get rid of this characteristic.
Spoon	To eat with one: See what you can do to improve your overall health. To see a silver one: Don't spend your money on things you don't really need.
Sporting gun	To see one: Change your opinions or you will get yourself into trouble. To have one: Unless you are very careful, your enterprise will not succeed.
Spouse	To dream about your spouse means: Jealous people will try very hard to disrupt your relationship.

Spring

To see a clear one: You will have your share of the good things in life.

To take a bath in one: You can be sure that your projects will turn out well.

To drink out of one: Don't give up - your time will come and you will soon be lucky again.

To see one covered with ice: You may require a lot of courage if you are to complete your project.

To see a dried-out one: Make your knowledge public.

To see one in a meadow: Good times are ahead. You will definitely reach your goal.

Spy

To dream about one: People may condemn you, but don't pay them any mind.

Square

You will be held responsible for the irregularities of others.

Squeak

To hear one: Take things a bit easier. Don't try to do so many things at once.

Squeeze

Something: Be patient if you want to reach your goal. First, you must get yourself organized.

Squinting

To see a person: Don't get into trouble with your neighbors. Avoid gossip.

Squirrels

To see them: What once seemed satisfactory may now appear to be insufficient.

To feed them: Access to confidential information smooths the path.

Stabbed

To be stabbed: You can count on a long life.

To see someone get stabbed: Diplomacy should dominate the negotiations. If you use tact rather than force, you will surely be the victor.

Stable

To see one: An acquaintance considers you as a friend.

To see one with horses in it: Don't try to deal with business situations that you do not fully comprehend.

To see one burning: You will only become wealthy if you work hard.

Stable boy

To see one: You may be involved in helping to resolve a dispute.

Stag

To see one standing: A member of the opposite

	sex will make an important contact for you. To see one run: Short trips can be beneficial, for both business and pleasure.
Stage	To see a ballet: You are not motivated by honest thoughts.
Stage coach	To dream of one: You shoulder great responsibility.
Stagger	Out of bed: You involve yourself in unnecessary danger. Staggering down a mountain: A mistake could ruin your reputation.
Staircase	To fall down one: Don't pay any attention to the rumors around you. To walk up one: You have to fight to secure your means of livelihood. To descend one: After a strenuous time, you will live comfortably.
Stallion	To see one: Cut down on unnecessary expenditures to make good a recent loss.
Stamp collection	To see one: As your efforts are useless, it is best to use your energy elsewhere.
Stamps	To see them on an envelope: Good news will come from afar.
Starlings	To see them fly: Don't gossip - it will surely backfire. To feed them: Someone will try to betray you, because you are good-hearted.
Stars	To see them shining bright in the sky: Unexpected events could upset your plans. To see them as small and fading: It is difficult to negotiate favorable agreements right now. To see one falling from the sky: Your talents will make a lasting impression on a person in a position of authority.
Starving	To see yourself starving in your dream means: Someone will try to give you a hard time.
Statistician	Don't be so sincere; you could easily be caught in an embarrassing situation.
Statue	To see one: Your plans will advance rapidly due

	to the fact that there are no obstacles which could interfere.
Steal	To see yourself stealing: A family secret will be discussed in an atmosphere of privacy.
Steam	To see it travel upwards: Use your imagination to solve a tricky problem. To see it inside the house: You have enemies, however, they are not dangerous.
Steamboat	To see a small one: An unexpected, enjoyable weekend vacation is in sight. To see a large one: You may embark upon a long journey, one that may turn out to be complicated. To be on one: Your plan will be completed in half the time you allotted yourself to accomplish it.
Steam-engine	To repair one: More haste, less speed.
Steamtrain	To be seated in one: Quite accidentally, you could find yourself face to face with someone you have long admired.
Steel	To see it: You discover a secret.
Steeple	To dream about one: Save your strength for a better time.
Step-ladder	To ascend one: You will feel confident and will be able to pursue your ambitions. To descend one: Some sort of showdown is indicated.
Step parents	To speak to them: Don't reach for the stars they are too far away.
Stepsister	To see her: People don't recognize your true nature.
Stick	To have a stick in your dream foretells that your sweetheart is unfaithful to you.
Still	To own one: Don't delay a moment longer. The chances that your expectations will be successful right now are very good.
Stilts	To see somebody walking on them: Be open-minded, but not gullible.

Stirrups	To see them on a horse: Be cautious in your ventures.
Stitch	You will receive an invitation to a banquet.
Stocks	To buy them: Don't worry quite so much; everything can be straightened out.
Stockfish	To eat: Be prepared for a change.
Stocktaking	To do: Your faith in programs and in people is vindicated.
Stockings	To buy them: Pay off debts as early as possible, in order to avoid trouble with creditors. To see slim legs with ragged stockings: Your judgment is not always fair and impartial. To wash them: Regret the things you have done in the past.
Stomach	To see a big one: This is a good time to plan a surprise outing for the entire family. To have a stomach pain: With a little bit of careful thought, you may have a permanent relationship.
Stones	To see them: You will make a successful adjustment. To break them: Your efforts will be crowned with victory.
Stonemason	To see one at work: Speculation must be avoided. Otherwise, you could lose your money.
Stool	To stand on one: Your spouse is faithful to you.
Store	To see one with customers: Your trade will bring you a lot of success. To buy something in a store: Be careful - you will have a loss in the future. To see a closed one: Tackle a financial or legal problem today and you will emerge the victor. To see one: Be careful that you don't take a loved one for granted.
Storks	To see them in a nest: Be careful, or people will try to steal from you. To see them: Your behavior is not at its best right now and could cause you to lose some friends. To see them flying: Hard work brings its own rewards.

To hear them chirping: You will lose your pride, and then you will fall.

Storm
To hear one: Enmity at home.
To witness one: If people seem unfair to you right now, don't pay them any mind. You may have desperate need of them in the future.

Storm lantern
To see or carry one: You will now separate illusions from facts and will consequently find yourself on the road to solid achievement.

Story
To hear one: Your plans will be fruitful if you stick with your destiny.
To tell one: Unless you are honest in the first place, you could put yourself in a very embarrassing situation later on when you are called upon to correct yourself.

Stout
To be stout: You have a lot of rethinking to do with regards to food and diet.

Stove
To see one glow: Sometimes your friends find it difficult to comprehend your behavior.
To touch a cold one: Money discussions at home will seem never-ending.

Stove pipe
To see one: You will be hurt, but only slightly.

St. Peter
To dream about him means: A health problem must be handled very carefully.

Straightjacket
To see one in your dream: Routine tasks command more than the usual amount of attention.

Stranger
To see one: This is not a very favorable time to conduct business.

Strangled
To be strangled means: An unlucky omen.

Stratosphere aircraft
To take part in: If you are unattached and have recently met someone to whom you are attracted, take steps to make the association more meaningful.

Straw
To see one: Your enterprise will be impeded.

Strawberries
To eat them: A longstanding project will be completed.
To pick them: You are too arrogant to be profitable in business.

Straw hat	To wear one: People will honor you because of the courage you have shown.
Stream	To see a long one: Home and family affairs offer the opportunity for some good luck. To see a torrential one: Speculation could cause you to suffer a serious loss.
Street	With people on it: You will become annoyed with the authorities. To see an empty one: You will have to use a great deal of tolerance and patience if you want to avoid quarrels with relatives. To see a broad one: An important activity should be postponed for the time being.
Stretcher	To lie on one: This is not the best time to start a new project. To see one: Unless more energy is expended, you may not obtain the results you desire.
String	Of pearls: Unless you change your attitude now, there will be difficult days ahead. To see a golden one: You will be honored and decorated in the near future. To see a silver one: Your hopes will probably be fulfilled if you remain close with your family. To see the strings of a violin: Don't communicate with people who are only interested in your money. To see the strings of a harp: Where danger is involved, something exciting will occur.
String music	To hear it: After a long separation, a lost love could be recovered.
Student	To see one: A family reunion will bring you pleasure.
Submarine	To dream about one means: You will be on the right side of a secret.
Successor	A relative who offers you advice, however sincere he may appear to be, could be misinformed.
Suffocated	To see somebody: Your present unfortunate situation won't last for much longer. To see yourself: You have a change in mind but you're not too sure where to begin.

Sugar
To eat some: Make sure that your body receives all of the required nutrients.

Suicide
To commit: Ignore anyone with a jealous streak.

Suit
To wear one: An early morning argument could start off the day with you in a bad mood.

Suitcase
To see one: This is a favorable time to take a long journey.
To buy one: You should be able to work on a special request.

Sulphur
To see it burn: After a long period of strife, your troubles will fade away.
To smell it: Numerous opportunities are present. Make the most of them.

Summer lightning
To see it in your dream: Deal diplomatically with those who have information that you need.

Sun
To see the sun rise: A death in your family.
To see it in the sky: You will be offered a government job.
To see a sunset: Be happy that everything is going the way you want it to.
To see the sun and the moon at the same time: For once and for all, you will know where a current romance is headed.

Sundial
To see one: Your struggle is unsuccessful.

Sunflowers
To see them: You have peace of mind. Try to keep things this way.

Sunshades
To buy them: Let others know of your individual skills and strong credentials.
To see them: Your business may stagnate, but don't give up. Try a little harder.

Supper
To eat out: A major domestic adjustment will dominate the next few months.

Surgeon
To see one: The disappointment you have felt lately will be transformed into a positive asset.

Surgical instruments
To see them: Keep on the lookout for better connections.

Surprise
To be surprised: You must have more confidence in your abilities.

Swaggerer
To listen to one: Your partner or spouse will object if you pay too much attention to your work.

Swallows
To see them in a nest: What once seemed out of reach is now within your grasp.
To see them flying high in the sky: You have a secret delight.
To see many of them: This is your lucky day, one in which you may receive important news.

Swamp
To see one: You could have an advantage if you concentrate on property and domestic issues.

Swans
To see a couple of them: Be diplomatic and discreet and remember not to cast the first stone.
To see a swan die: Think twice before agreeing to go on a journey.
To see a black swan: You have a happy marital life.

Swear
To swear an oath: Your investments will yield large returns.

Sweat
To feel it on yourself: There is danger of an accident if you allow your mind to wander.
To see it on someone else: Be on the lookout for the people in your neighborhood.

Sweeping
The floor: Although they don't show it, some of your acquaintances are jealous of you.
The street: Don't let others assume responsibility for your money.

Sweetheart
To dream about him or her: Plans you wish to implement are likely to get the thumbs-down sign.

Swimming
To swim and reach your goal: You will be honored.
To swim and not reach your goal: Envious people surround you.
To swim in choppy water: A special negotiation will be successful for you.
To swim and dive: Be smart in order to be successful.
To swim and struggle with a fish: You will finish rather than initiate a project.
To swim with people from a shipwreck: Somebody will try to entrap you.
To swim beside a boat: You will receive all the help you need.

To swim in high waves: Control your temper.
To swim in clear water: Your proposal will involve a lot of hard work.
To swim in dirty water: You will be punished for your wrongdoings.
To see children swimming: Your desire comes true.

Swimming pool   To see one: Try to prevent an accident.
Also, beware of burglars.

Swindle   To do: Don't spread false rumors.

Swine   To see one: Your mind is heading in the wrong direction.

Swing   To sit in one: The present pleasure will be short-lived.
To see one: Express your individuality when dealing with the people around you.

Swing bridge   To see one: A change of pace is necessary.
Watch your health.

Switch   To see one: Welcome the opportunity to have a little more breathing space.
To break one: This means trouble and distress.

Sword   To hold one in your hand: Happiness and honor will only come to you if you stay on the straight and narrow path.
To lose one: You will never experience poverty if you keep your current job.
To see one: Although your visitors will be unpleasant, they will give you some valuable information.
To pull one and fight: You will be endangered if you follow the advice of a so-called friend.
If you get cut by one: Try to rid yourself of some of your bad habits.
To carry one: You will hear of a very hurtful insult.
To touch a sword blade: You will be contacted by quarrelsome people.
To see a broken one: Someone's death brings you grief and regrets.

Sword fight   To see one: Don't be a workaholic. You need rest from time to time, too.

Sword knot   To see one: A friendly family will move away.

Synagogue	To see one: You have the chance to learn something which could be very important to your future success.
Syringe	To see one: Days of happiness are not too far away.
Syrup	To eat some: Refuse to give up something for nothing in return.

Table

If you see an ordinary one: Your financial future will be bright.
To set a table: There could be a sudden disagreement with your mate or partner within the next couple of days.
If you see one with a spoiled cloth on: Don't give up hope. Times will improve.
If you see a very big or long one: Sometimes you try to hide your past.
With people sitting on a table: Save money as well as you can, as you may have need of it to settle your business.

Table-cloth

To see one: Enmity and jealousy will follow you.

Tadpole

To see or touch one: Don't panic about a perception you will make in the next few days.

Tail

If you have one in a dream: This means luck and happiness.

Tailor

To see one working or to speak to one: Bizarre things are happening within your family.

Talisman

To wear one: The truth you will come to know will be surprisingly pleasant for you.

Talk

Make a speech: Someone will ask you to volunteer for something.
To hear a speech: This promises honor and fame.
If you talk to animals or if they should talk to you: You will find that loved ones and friends are right behind you all the way.

Tallow

To see or work with it: Beware, for somebody is trying very hard to bring you harm.

Tambourine

To see or use one: Any investments you make right now could turn out to be favorable.

Taming

If you try to: Unless you tell others about your sorrow, you cannot expect them to comfort you.

Tank

If you see a watertank or any other sort of tank in your dream: You will be more successful than you expected to be.

Tanner

To see one or to see something being tanned: You can't escape your destiny.

Tab room

To sit in one: Be good to your wife. She loves you dearly.

Tapestry	To see one: You are sensitive, unusually emotional and you have strong family ties.
Tapeworm	If you see or have one in a dream: Be careful about becoming entangled in affairs which could very easily end up in a court of law.
Tar	To see or work with it: Pay more attention to matters of a personal nature. To see it on fire: You will receive some money unexpectedly.
Tarantula	If you see this spider in your dream: The only way to escape your enemies is to change your residence.
Target	To see one: Don't gamble with money that you can't afford to lose.
Tassel	Of gold: Your business success is decreasing. Of any other material: Your business may improve if you try to be more reliable.
Tatter	To collect it: Your speculations will likely prove to be successful.
Tattoo	To be tattooed: If you become involved with the law, you stand a chance of losing your freedom. To see tattoos on others: Your vanity may drive your lover away.
Taurus	To see: Small quarrels within your family will arise. To be chased by one: Power and courage are the key to your success. To see one slaughtered: With a little good will, you will make it. If you see one with long horns: Watch out. In a pasture: You will receive a letter.
Tavern	To be in one: Be aware of your passions, as they could quite conceivably destroy you.
Taxes	If you pay taxes in a dream: Your rivals would like nothing better than to give you a bad reputation. Fight back.
Tea	To make some: Begin a new savings strategy. To drink some: An abrupt change at work could cause some uncomfortable moments. If you see a cup of tea in your dream, but find

yourself unable to drink it: If you were more modern you would obtain better results.

Teapot   To see one: Where investments are concerned, you would be wise to be cautious.

Teacher   If you see one or if one is talking to you: Sometimes, you tend to act like a fool.
If you speak to one: Bring your letter writing up to date.

Tears   If you cry: A great pleasure is in store for you.
To see someone cry: Don't rely heavily on the plans of others.
Work hard to save.

Technician   To be one or to see one: You will not be asked to work overtime without compensation.

Teenager   To see or talk to one: Make more of an effort to please close members of the family.
Happy times will follow disappointments.

Teeth   To wear or receive false teeth: You will soon be back on the right track, because you are confident of your actions.
To become teeth in a dream: Your wishes will come true.
To have teeth pulled out: Beware of jealous people.
If your teeth fall out: A person close to you will die.
To get a filling: People will envy you.
If you have pearly white teeth in a dream: Take care of your health.
If you see gold ones in your mouth: You will have success.
If you are brushing your teeth: You may sustain a loss.
If you have a toothache in a dream: A problem will arise shortly, one which you are not able to cope with alone.
If you have loose teeth in a dream: This is a bad omen.
If you see someone with beautiful teeth: Your diligence will be duly recognized and rewarded.

Telegram   To receive one: Family problems warrant immediate attention.

	To send one: Your cheerfulness makes everyone happy. This can also mean that there is some kind of disturbance at work.
Telephone	To see one: Unexpected visitors are unwelcome. To dial one: People who work behind the scenes will bring you joyful tidings. If you receive a telephone call in a dream: Be careful not to lose your money. To hear a telephone ring: Attention - there is a danger of fire.
Telescope	To see through one: You will discover the secret of a family member.
Temple	To be in or see one: Adopt a give-and-take attitude.
Temptation	To give in to: Misery and envy surround you.
Tenpin	If you bowl it in a dream: You have a dependable friend in whom you can trust.
Tent	To see or be in one: Your next trip will be pleasant and delightful. To pitch one: You will make it to the top without the help of others.
Terrace	If you see or sit in one: You should be fairly pleased with the results that you will obtain in the near future.
Terrestrial globe	To see one: This means that you should be careful when dealing in matters of real estate. Have more faith in the advice of experts.
Terror	If you have this feeling in a dream: This promises of a new career offer.
Testament	To make: You may mourn a next of kin.
Testicle	To see one: You will gain the advantage.
Thanks	To thank someone: This reminds you not to forget to say thank-you.
Thanksgiving	To celebrate it: Don't always look up; look down sometimes. If you do, you may realize that you are well off.
Thatch roof	To see one: Be cautious of fire hazards.

Theater   To be in one and to see the stage of one: You may be involved in an accident - be careful.
If you are an actor on the stage: Team work pays handsomely.

Thermometer   To read one: You will be severely tested.

Thief   To see one: Your hopes are beyond the realms of reality.
To catch one: Don't condemn people who you do not really know.
To be a thief: Be aware of bad advice or false friends.
To see a pickpocket or to be a victim of one: If you are truthful and outspoken, you will be helped.

Thimble   To see or wear one: Unpleasantness with your next of kin.

Thirst   To quench it: Your satisfaction will be short-lived.
To be thirsty and have nothing to drink: You are on the brink of completing your project.

Thistle   To see one: Times of worry and strife will soon come to an end.
To be cut or injured by one: Take your time to sort out unresolved problems. They will not go away by themselves.

Thorns   To see a hedge with thorns: If you are friendly to an unfriendly neighbor, he will change his attitude.
To see rose thorns: Give special attention to the fine print.

Thousand   To see this number in a dream: Romance will remain happy as long as you guard against casual alliances.

Thrash   To see somebody doing it: Nothing is as important as making your feelings known now.

Thread   To see or to work with some: Don't let your family suffer because you have to reach a deadline. Don't worry - you will make it.

Threaten   Threatening someone: Regret an injustice and make peace with your family and neighbors.

To feel threatened in a dream: This is a warning to be cautious of accidents and sickness.

Threatening letter   If you receive such a letter in a dream: Be aware of pretentious persons. Their only interest is to harm you.

Threshing floor   This year's harvest will satisfy you.

Throat   To touch someone's throat: Enemies will triumph over you.
To see or touch your own: If ill, you should be able to get some relief from a specialist.

Throne   To sit on one: Shortly you will realize that practice is better than theory.

Throstle   To hear this bird sing: Now you will find out who is really on your side.

Thumb   To see yours or somebody else's: Circumstances favor your efforts.
To dream of fingers with an impressive thumb: This reveals strength and indicates that the undertaking ahead of you will be successfully accomplished as a result of your skill.

Thunder   To hear it: A happy reunion with an old friend.

Thunderstorm   If you witness a thunderstorm during your dream: Trouble is heading your way.

Ticket   To receive and hold one in your hand: Your ability to remain calm under pressure will not help alleviate the difficult situation you are in.

Tickled   To be: You can probably avoid doing harm to another person.

Ticks   To see them crawling: Don't pay any attention to the obstinacy of your peers.
To mash one: Trouble on the job or in your business.

Tiger   To see one: An unknown enemy won't give you any peace until you find out who it is and have a confrontation.

Tightrope walker   To see one: Take advantage of any opportunities to which you may be able to lend a helping hand.
To be one: Drive carefully and obey all traffic regulations.

Tiled stove To see one: There is a chance of an engagement.
To heat one: Try to rest as much as possible in
your spare time.

Till To see one: This is a good omen and signifies
luck in love.

Tiller To work with one: Your life may not be easy,
but try not to complain. The people around you
have fond feelings for you. If you remember
this, your existence will seem that much more
worthwhile.

Timber To see some: Any impulsive financial moves you
make are almost certain to result in loss.
To see people working with timber: Good luck
in business affairs.

Tin If you see a pewter vessel: A promotion at work
is a distinct possibility.

Tip To give one: Look for additional ways to trim
your budget.

Tissue paper If you handle it in your dream: Somebody will
surprise you with a beautiful gift.

Titmouse If you see this small bird in your dream: You
should choose the lesser of two evils.

Toad To see one: Your happiness at home is only temporary.

Tobacco To smoke it: Take good care of your reputation.
To sniff it: Bad luck on all fronts.
To chew it: Unstable love life.

Tobacco pipe To see or smoke one: The way in which you are
in control of your job right now is likely to
make an excellent impression on your boss.

Toboggan To ride one: You will reach your goal very soon.

Tocsin To hear: A legal matter or news of a divorce
may come soon.

Toes To see your own: You like to do your own thing,
but sometimes you would be better off to follow
the advice of elderly, experienced people.
To see the toes of somebody else: Your dreams
will be shattered unless you are more reserved.

Toll	To pay one: A candid appraisal of your business or career is necessary right now.
Tomatoes	To eat or see them: This means good health. It can also signify a secret love affair.
Tombstone	To see one: A blessed marriage and well-being. To see many in a cemetery: It would be extremely unwise to share innovative ideas with those who are not directly involved.
Tomcat	To see one: Someone will try to make you waiver about an important matter. Don't listen to them.
Tongue	To see one: A forgotten friend is anxious to attract attention.
Tools	To see or to have some: Do everything in your power to improve the atmosphere at home.
Toothpick	To see or to use one: Your present behavior is not conducive to success.
Topcoat	To see or wear one: Your health is of the utmost importance. Therefore, you should take excellent care of it.
Torch	To carry one: Somebody loves you, but you are not yet aware of their feelings. To see one: An important matter will be clarified to you.
Torch bearer	To see one: You will receive honor later in life.
Torment	If you are tormented: One way or another, in the future you will have to show more strength.
Tornado	To witness one: Unexpected events have the potential of causing serious upsets.
Torpedo	To see one: A very beneficial change is about to occur.
Torrent	If you see a torrent in the mountains: Be prepared for test questions.
Torture	You see somebody being tortured: Don't allow accidents to happen. To be tortured: Keep an eye on evil people. To witness torture with a crowd of people: Your success will leave you.

Tourist

To be one: Promises that your hopes will be fulfilled.
To see one: Express your views, but also show that you are willing to listen to the opinions of others.

Tournament

To see one: Someday, you will have a prestigious job.

Tower

To see a large one: Before signing contracts, you may require additional information.
To ascend the stairs of a tower: Look behind the scenes.

Town hall

To see it from the exterior: If in trouble, seek help from those who have proven to be helpful in the past.
If you are inside and unable to find a room: Be honest with yourself and stop resisting.
If you work in the town hall: You will be honored in your profession.

Toy

To play with one: Don't allow others to suppress you.

Trace

To follow a trace in a dream: You will have a discussion with an enemy. If you are nice, you will claim victory.

Trade

To conduct trading in a dream: You will receive a message which could bring success.

Traffic accident

To have one in your dream: A candid discussion with your spouse will give you peace of mind.

Tragedy

To hear of: Means grief and distress.

Train (of a dress)

To wear one: You should focus on production and promotion.

Train engine

To see one in motion: A change of address will provide you with a better lifestyle.

Train station

To see one at a distance: If you push your luck, you will impede your progress.
If the dreamer is at the station: Don't toy with the idea of moving to another state; you have many opportunities right where you are.

Traitor

If you see one or hear of one in a dream: As your worries are increasing, the only way out is through negotiation.

Tramp	To see one: Your future does not look prosperous.
Trap	To see one: You will be harmed. To set a trap: Be happy that you escaped a dangerous situation. To be caught in one: It never rains, but it pours. Take comfort - your situation will improve in a little while.
Trapdoor	To see one: Your fears are groundless. It is safe to be a little bit more courageous.
Trapeze	If you have a sick friend and you see a trapeze in a dream: Your friend will soon be healthy again.
Travelling companion	To have one: This warns you that your hopes will be crushed.
Tray	To carry one: This means that your point of view will be recognized. Your income will remain reliable and stable.
Treason	If you are guilty of treason in a dream: A long term relationship could suddenly change.
Treasure	To find one in a dream: You are now capable of discerning long range possibilities.
Tree-frog	To see one: Arguments could break out over silly, unimportant things.
Tree nursery	To be in one: If you follow your original decision, your hopes will be fulfilled.
Trees	If you see or walk through a forest: Your loneliness was a normal situation for you for a while, but now you are once again looking for companionship. You will soon meet somebody and this will make you a very happy person. To plant a tree: Don't lose touch with friends and acquaintances - everyone needs someone to communicate with. To see a fruit tree bearing fruit: The influence of friends very often points you in the wrong direction. To see a tree in blossom: You are aware of the differences between the important and the unimportant matters in your life. This realization is one of the reasons for your success. To see a tree without leaves or to see a dead tree:

You will suffer misfortune; perhaps a loss of money, a decline in business, or unemployment.
To climb a tree in a dream: Don't ever give up on your goal. It may take some time, but you will eventually reach your destination.
If you fall from a tree: Don't be so anxious - your sickness is not a lethal one.
To cut a tree: Your wanton ways will eventually hurt you.

Trefoil   To pick: The times ahead will be hard ones, but you will survive and prosper.

Trellis   To see one: You will hear different news.

Tremble   If you tremble in a dream: Blame the time and circumstances, not yourself, for the critical situation you find yourself in now.

Tress   To see or wear one: You will suffer personal damage.
If you see a very long one: You are not as smart as you pretend to be.

Trial   To hear one: Hold on tightly to your family.
To be involved in one: Rid yourself of any feelings of anger.

Triangle   If you see one somewhere in your dream: This image tells you that protectors are on your side.

Tricycle   To ride or see one: You can count on additions to the family.

Trimming   To see a gold trimming: Unless you change, your pride will suffer.
A silver trimming: A testament will be made to your advantage.

Trip   If you dream of taking a trip: You will once again come into contact with distant enemies.

Triplets   To see them: A happy occasion is on the way.
To see newly born triplets in a dream: Someone loves you very much.
This image can also foretell a very happy marriage.

Tripod   To see a tripod: This can mean that you will have a very happy home and family life. You will also have a very good marriage.

Trombone	To blow one: A newly formed friendship will be short lived.
Trophy	To receive one: Promises of enjoyment, luck and happiness. To see somebody receive one: A gift from a close friend will surprise you.
Tropical forest	To see one: You tend to become inextricably involved in personal matters.
Trough	To see or use one: An unwelcome, unwanted visitor will come. You should tell him face to face how you see the situation.
Trousers	If you see a pair of trousers in a dream: This is a warning that your spouse may become ill. To wear some yourself: This means that although your love life may be troubled, it is within your power to fix it. To wear ragged ones: Good humor and happiness will never leave your life.
Trout	To catch one: Good luck is just around the corner. To eat one: Take advantage of all opportunities forthcoming within the next few weeks.
Trowel	To see or work with one: A telephone conversation will lead to misunderstandings.
Truck	To see one: Accomplish your proposal. To drive one: Be honest and don't try to cheat others. This can also mean that you will be somewhat lucky.
Trumpets	To hear or see them: A major domestic adjustment is due.
Tub	To have a bath: If you are continually on the alert, you will save a lot of money. To see one: A bad omen for your business or employment.
Tuesday	To dream about: The future is looking good.
Tulips	If you see some in a field: It is possible that you will change your occupation. To pick some: Somebody whom you will meet will aid in removing the obstacles to success.
Tumble	To see somebody: A safety device could prove to be a great asset.

If you tumble on flat ground: Your wishes will come true.
In a ditch: People speak ill of you.
To tumble and hold on to something: Good times are on the way.
To be injured while tumbling: You are involved, whether you are aware of it or not.
To tumble from a high place: You will have bad luck in gambling.

Tumult   To see or witness one: Don't allow relatives to drain your reserves.

Tunnel   To pass through one: This is a very good omen for you. Have trust in your fate.

Turf   To see a very green one: Search the neighborhood if you have the intention of buying a new home.

Turkeys   To see some: You will have access to confidential information.
To eat turkey meat: You will hear some bad news connected to politics.

Turkish bath   To be in one: Before you begin the new project, you will think it over thoroughly.
To see another take a bath in one: Make your life a little easier - try not to be so jealous.

Turner's workshop Your wish will be fulfilled, but not in the manner you originally anticipated.

Turnip   To see or eat one: Be aware of troubles in your workplace.

Turn lathe   To see or work on one: Keep calm if something · should go wrong.
Think first, before you give your opinion.

Turnpike   To see one: You may have to choose between freedom and security.

Turpentine   To buy or smell it: You must straighten something out.

Turtle   To see one: You have a tendency to stray from the truth.

Turtle-doves   To see some: Refuse to be cajoled into making hasty decisions.

	To see them fly: The time for revision and review is now.
Tweezers	To work with some: Your work is without success.
Twig	To see one in your dream: Your prestige will rise, you will be widely recognized and a burden will be lifted.
Twilight	If you have the feeling of dusk in a dream: It is your physical condition which has been giving you cause for concern. Perhaps you should see a doctor.
Twins	If you see twins in your dream: This always means happiness.
Typewriter	To use one: Unpleasant things will be cleared up. To see someone else using one: There is no excuse for your laziness. You should pull yourself together.

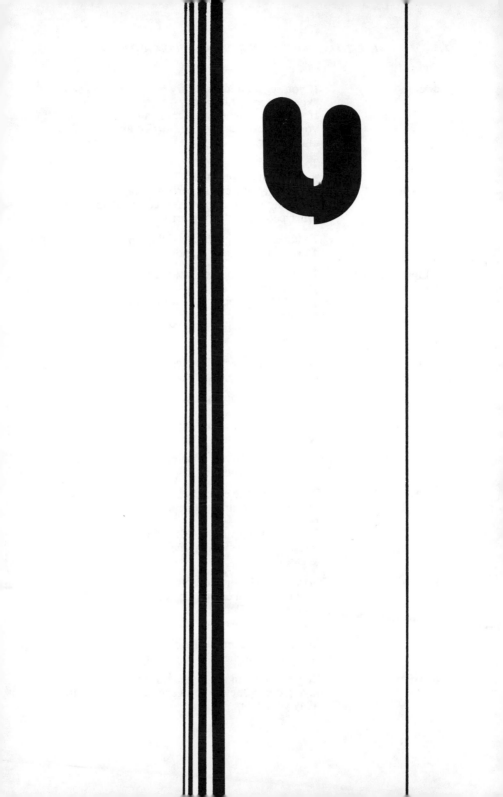

Udder
If you see an udder and try to milk it: You can expect an enormous gift.
If you see somebody touching an udder: Means you will never have to be worried about food and shelter.

Ugly
To see yourself ugly: Your lasting embarrassment turns people away.
To see ugly objects in a dream: Your disagreement and opposition in your conversations with other people leads to quarrels.

Ulcer
To have one: A good friendship will break up.
To see one: Means a standstill in business.

Umbrella
To carry one: You would have more success if you were more polite.
To see other people with umbrellas: You will be honored.
To see one torn to pieces: You are surely in need for help.

Unbind
To untie or detach: Foretells of a troublesome time.

Uncle
To see him: People get you into difficult situations.
To see your uncle with other people: Watch out for swindlers.

Unconscious
To see somebody or yourself in a dream: Unexpected inheritance.

Undressed
To see someone else: Protect your assets, expand your horizons, and dig beneath surface indications.
To see yourself undressed: Your intellectual interests will keep you on the go in the months ahead.

Uniform
To see one: Be gracious and diplomatic when dealing with an elderly person.
To wear one: People with problems find themselves drawn to you.

Union
To dream of a union: Don't be so sure that co-workers are as helpful as you are.

University
To see one from the outside: It would be worth laying out money to see a specialist in order to allay your fears.

To be in one or be a student at one: Any extra cash that comes your way should be saved, not spent, because of possible financial difficulties in the future.

University lecturer   Many persons sensing your vulnerability are only too willing to take advantage.

Unload   To unload something: Need and grief befall acquaintances or friends.

Unlucky   If you are unlucky in a dream: Always keep in mind; the early bird gets the worm.

Unsaddle   Don't think of retirement yet; your health will improve and you will discern that work is the best medicine.

Uranium   To find some: Communication with close relatives will give you a brand new idea which may lead to success.

Urine   To pass: Someone may try to start a quarrel. Ignore it.
To spill: You will be faced with new challenges and restrictions.
To see some on a street: Think about your honesty.
To step in some: Unexpected luck.
To smell some: Prestige swings upwards. This is a good time for you.

Urn   To see a broken one: Misery comes over you.

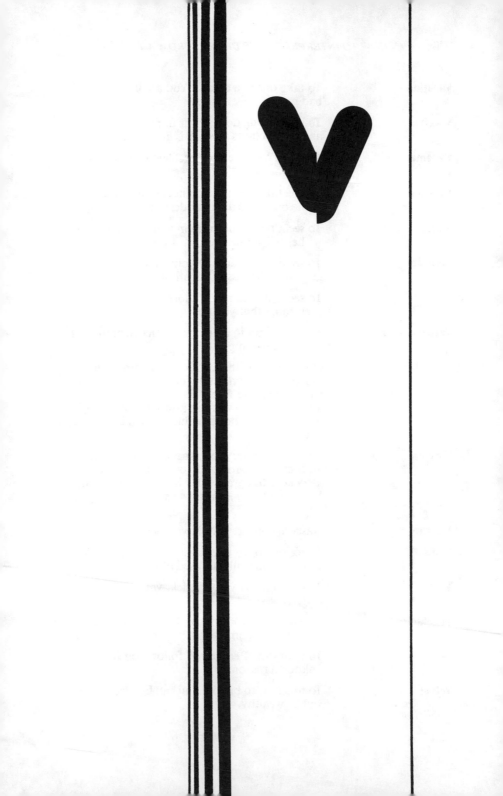

Vacation	To take one in a dream: You are involved with bad gossip.
Vaccinate	To see it being done: Your unpleasant feeling about infectious diseases is groundless.
Vademecum	To have: You are very intelligent, so why do you act so foolish.
Vagrant	To meet one: Your happiness is unstable. To be one: You are in undesirable company.
Valley	To see a beautiful valley in a dream: All your wishes will come true.
Vampire	To see one: Because of your kindness you will get into a distressful situation.
Vapor	To see in a dream: Put more effort into everything that you do.
Varicose veins	To have them in a dream: An accident in your family may happen.
Varnishing	If you work with varnish in a dream: You will only receive ingratitude for things you have done with proud and free will. To see someone working: Importunate people will ask you to do something which is against your morals.
Vase	To see one: Everybody speaks well of you. To break one: You will not be able to get associates to agree with what you are offering. With flowers in it: You will get an invitation to a party.
Vatican	Nasty assaults do not have any affect on you.
Vault	To see one or to put something in a vault: You will be wrongfully accused of something.
Veal	To eat some: If you are sick, you will soon feel better.
Vegetables	To eat some: You will get a letter which you have waited a long time for.
Veil	To wear one: People will follow you for an unknown reason.
Velvet	To touch or to buy it: You can be sure that you will be wealthy.

Venetian blinds	To see or to operate them: One who makes grandiose promises may not be in a position to fulfill them.
Vengeance	To take: Somebody will upset your calculations, and you will have to change your destiny.
Venus	To see this planet in your dream: You can impress those in charge if you do not panic when under fire.
Veranda	To sit in one: You will be better off if you do important things by yourself.
Verdict	To pass one: You are disputatious and people don't pay you any attention any more. Change your behavior. To read one: Attention to diet and nutrition is more important than might be imagined. Know it and act accordingly.
Vermicelli	To eat them: Try to keep ahead of your opponents.
Vest	To wear one: Make it a habit to always be friendly to people.
Vibrate	You will learn where you stand with a special person.
Vicar	To see or talk to one: Your knowledge provides you with a big opportunity.
Victory	To achieve: Short but pleasant hours, although very expensive ones.
View	A pretty view: A burden will be lifted. A cloudy view: Through your own fault you experience poverty.
Village	To see one in your dream: Don't make inconsiderate decisions. To walk through a village: You may get a wedding invitation. To see the village church: Your ambition to be somebody is so voluminous that you may start to tell lies.
Village inn	To sit in one: Think before you speak.
Village magistrate	To meet one: You may piece evidence together and claim victory.

Villager   To meet one: Be reserved when you attend the next party.

Vinegar   To see or to taste it: Major changes occur in the house.
To spill it: People will laugh at you because you are vain.
To smell it: Your opinions about saving will not be accepted by some family members.

Vineyard   To see a vineyard or to walk through one in a dream: A casual conversation with a stranger could give you food for thought.

Vintage   To see: Pleasure and comfort.
To attend: Do not poke your nose into other people's business.

Violets   To get them as a gift: Soon you will become engaged.
To pick them: You will meet your intended wife or husband sometime this year.
To see violets in a garden or in a field: Luck in love.

Violin   To hear or to play one: You will hear a bad discussion which may end up in court.
To see or hear a whole orchestra playing violins: Try to restore lost energy. Take a few days off work.

Viper   If you see one in a dream and become scared: If something bothers you speak out; it is the only way to clear the air.

Virginity   To lose it in a dream: What appeared to be a restriction could actually be a mere sign to be cautious.

Vision   From deceased persons: Means a prosperous change.
From deceased next of kin: You have a good opportunity right now and you will be successful if you continue.
Of objects: Oppose people who always try to hold you back.
Of children: You are in favor of an inheritance.
Of animals: Curb your passions.
Of ghosts: Look for the person who is gossiping about you.

Visit	If you open the door and a strange person stands in front of you: Your life will not be an easy one, but you will always manage to avoid poverty.
Voice	To hear one in a dream: Follow the advice of parents or good friends. To hear many voices: Happiness will continue for a longer period than expected.
Volcano	To see one in action: You have a chance to obtain a stronger position at your place of employment.
Vomiting	Yourself in a dream: A family member will tell you confidential information. To see somebody vomiting: Take life easier. Don't resist all the time.
Vote	To vote: You will find yourself in an embarrassing situation unless you don't change your attitude.
Voucher	To receive one: You will have a costly experience. To write one: Business affairs will be profitable if you don't make the drastic changes which you have in mind.
Voyage	To take one: You should avoid a curious person. This person is trying to discover a secret which you would like to keep.
Vulture	To see one flying: You will become acquainted with shallow untruthful people. To see one in a field: Forewarns a physical accident.

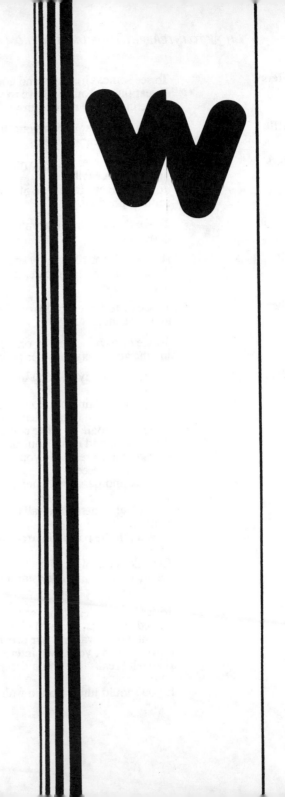

Wafers

To see some: Greetings and good news.
To eat them: You will have to visit your doctor sometime in the near future.

Waffle

If you see or eat one in your dream: It is time to change your eating habits.

Wages

To receive some: An unexpected settlement will make you very happy.
To give wages: Take care of financial matters as soon as possible.

Wagtail

To see this bird in a dream: This is a prophecy of good news.

Wait

If you wait for somebody or something in your dream: Unforeseen incidents will influence your life.

Waiter

To see or to be served by one: You may lose your independence.

Waitress

To see or to be served by one: Be wary of accepting the generosity of other people.

Walking

To see somebody walking in a dream: Luck is on the way.
If you are walking but don't seem to be getting anywhere: With despondency you will never reach your goal. Be more courageous.
If you walk and reach your destination: You are accustomed to reaching your goals, but you will not always succeed.
To walk and pass someone: You will live a long life.
To walk and thereby to fall down: Perform with caution.
To walk in the park: Have confidence in your wife.
To walk in the night: There will be barriers to negotiations of misunderstandings with partners in business or at home.

Wall

To see one: Unless you free yourself from outmoded concepts, you will suffer great losses.
To stand on a wall in your dream: Don't back down - protect your own interests.
If a wall breaks down in a dream: This is a bad omen.
If you should jump from a wall: If asked,

answer all of the questions truthfully. If you don't, you could find yourself in big trouble.

Walled in   If you see somebody: This means that bad news will come from afar.
Yourself: Your offence is not as serious as you think it is.

Wallet   To see or handle one: Don't reveal a secret which somebody has entrusted you with.
To find one: Take extra care of someone's belongings.
To lose a wallet in a dream: You are pursued by angry debtors who won't leave you alone.

Wallpaper   To work with it: Happiness will replace intrigue.

Walnuts   To eat or see them: Back away from the line of fire.

Walnut tree   If you see a green one: You will soon be married.

Waltz   To dance one: You will receive a gift from someone who desires something in return.

Wander   If you wander: Your efforts to achieve a better job will be handsomely rewarded.

War   To see or be in one: It may be dangerous to break the law. If you do, you will be punished.

Wardrobe   To see your own: Don't invest money to secure the speculative interests of another.
To see a closet full of clothes: The time is favorable for consultations with influential people.

Warehouse   If you find yourself in a warehouse in your dream: It would be wise to leave important moves and decisions until much later.

Warrantor   If you should co-sign for someone in a dream: This warns of a disagreement and subsequent break-up between friends.
If someone signs for you: Be careful how you invest your profits.

Warts   To see or to have some: An inactive project will suddenly become active again.

Wash-basin   If you see a clean one: You will be freed from a heavy burden.

Washing   Yourself: This is a sign of a small financial gain.

Wasp   To see one or more: An unexpected dissociation. To be stung by one: People always envy your strength.

Waste   Something in a dream: This dream reminds you to be economical and to abstain from extravagance.

Watch (keep)   Yourself: You will soon have a new enemy.

Watch   If you see a golden one: Someone wants to steal something from you. If you break one: A former friend will condemn you because of your jealousy.

Watch a fire   To see or sit and watch a fire: Make sure that you don't allow yourself to be swept along on the wave of other peoples' enthusiasm.

Watchman   To see one: Avoid veering far from the basic course. To talk to one: Don't let newspaper headlines alarm you.

Water   To see clear water in a dream: A new approach will bring the desired results. To see dirty water: Adultery may occur in your family. To see it boil: Watch your temperament. To spill some: Don't kid yourself about your financial situation. To swim in a small pool of water: The pressure somebody will put on you will make your life uneasy. To walk through it: Don't worry - your future looks bright. To be scalded with it: Don't forget! Small things now and then can be important. To walk on water in a dream: Nevertheless, you can claim victory. To see a waterfall: Although your neighbors are unfair to you, try to keep calm. To take a ride on the water: This image has a very good meaning. It means that you will receive joyful tidings.

To see a flood: If you don't lose your courage, you will definitely triumph over your enemies.
To see a water pitcher in your dream: Your kindness is often the cause of other peoples' happiness. Don't change.
To see a water glass: You will soon realize your goal in life.
To see a seaplane: You have a good reputation and peace of mind.

Waterfall
To see one: If you make the first move, romance will work out well.

Waterfowl
To see one or many: Be aware of the possibility of an accident.

Water-lily
You will have to attend a funeral.

Water nymph
If you see a beautiful one: You should be careful in your associations with women.
To see them dance: Don't burn yourself.

Wax
To see or work with wax in a dream: You will become a land-owner.
To see very white wax: This means that your health is in very good condition.

Wax museum
To visit one: You spend too much money on entertainment.

Wayfarer
To see a merry one: Your impending vacation will be very enjoyable and you will meet very nice people.

Weak
If you feel weak in a dream: Someone in your family will become ill.

Wealth
If in your dream you have the feeling that you are wealthy: Be aware of dangerous speculation.

Weapons
To see one: An older individual may be taking advantage of your reluctance to put your foot down.

Weasel
To see one: If you desire to change your location, make sure that your new home is as comfortable as your present one.

Weather
To have beautiful weather in a dream: You will be asked questions, therefore, you should be familiar with source material.

To have inclement weather: Your family should come first in your life.
Sunny weather: If you are ill, you will soon be healthy again.
Rainy weather: There are misunderstandings between family members.

Weather vane   If you see one on a roof: Pleasure will reduce the stress of your worries.

Weave   To see someone weaving something: The people you are dealing with are faithful.
To see yourself weaving: If you utilize your talents you will not suffer distress.

Web   To see one: An unusually exciting time is coming in the near future.
This is also a good time for romance.
To destroy one: Some of your friends will desert you.

Wedding   To be at a wedding: You will be held back and, consequently, you will lose an opportunity.
To dance at one: On your next shopping trip, you should keep an eye open for pickpockets.
To see one from a distance: You are winning the heart of someone without really trying.

Wedding band   To see or to wear one: Older family members will share with you the benefits of their experience.

Weeds   To pick them: You have to overcome some barriers, but don't ask for any help. If you do, people will laugh at you.

Wet   To be: This warns you to be aware of the fact that not all people are honest.

Whale   To see one in the water: Your energy allows you to overcome present and future barriers.

Whalebone   To see one: You will receive joyful tidings. This news will give you a lot of strength.

Wharf   If you see one in your dream: This time, your hopes are too high and unrealistic.

Wheat   To see wheat in large amounts: Although "no exit" signs appear, there are ways to resolve the dilemma.

Wheel   To see a wheel in a dream: This is a good omen which can mean success in your business.

Wheelbarrow   To push one: Make your travel plans now if you
                       plan to visit a friend or relative.

Whip   To see somebody get whipped: You will be
                       disappointed by the action of a family member
                       against you.

Whipping post   To see somebody tied to one: If you are wealthy,
                       you will lose something. If you are poor, you
                       will make a good profit.

Whirlpool   To see or to have a bath in one: You will get into
                       trouble because of your own carelessness.

Whisky   To drink it in a dream: The offer you have made
                       will not be accepted.
                       To see some in a bottle: Don't treat your friends
                       with selfishness.
                       To buy some: Your family will be on your side if
                       you tell them the truth.

Whistle   To hear one in a dream: Somebody will warn
                       you, keep this in mind.

White people   If you see many white people in one place:
                       Don't let yourself be used by so-called friends
                       who only have their own interests in mind.

Widow   To see a widow in your dream: This is a sign that
                       you will learn about limitation.

Wife   If you see the wife of somebody else: You will
                       obtain a high status in your community.

Wig   To see one: Someone will try to suppress you.
                       If you wear a wig in a dream: Foretells of fame
                       and honor.

Wild duck   If you hunt them: Arguments or quarrels can
                       erupt over money matters.

Wilderness   If you walk through the wilderness: This is a
                       good time to come to terms with loved ones.

Will   If you make one in a dream: A family member
                       will strain your patience.

Will-o'-the-wisp   To see one: If you learn more about the project
                       you are handling right now you will be more
                       successful.

Windmill   Use your own original ideas to progress.

Window   To see a closed window in a dream: Be careful
                       -insincere friends will try to betray you.

To see an open window: Bad luck in your venture.

Window screen

To see or to try to fix one: People are hiding something from you.

Wine

To see the storage of wine bottles: You will be getting an invitation to an incredibly big party.
To drink red wine: From time to time you should make a compliment to a person you like a lot.
To drink white wine in a dream: Offer resistance to somebody.
To spill wine: You will destroy your own luck if you are not careful in your expression.

Wine cask

To see one: In the near future you may have visitors from a far away place.

Wine glass

To break one: Let reason, not impulse, be your guide.

Wink

To see someone wink: You should smile if you meet your adversary. Don't show what you are thinking.

Winning

Winning in a game: You really may have some luck in a lottery.

Winter

If it is winter in a dream: Your impatience with old methods could cause a confrontation with your partner.

Wire

To be tangled in wire: Be aware of loose talk and try to protect yourself from it.
To see electric wire: Better to proceed even though plans look bad.
To see rusty wire: One who appeared glamorous will now seem ordinary.

Wire basket

To carry one: Your doings will be hidden from the world, but occasionally you will get into trouble.

Wire fence

To see one: What appeared to be a solid connection may actually be unstable.

Witch

To see one: Be very careful when driving.

Witness

To be one in court: You are now able to locate an article that had been lost, missing or stolen.

Wizard	To see one: An unexpected event will occur.
Wolves	To see them: You must be extremely careful in what you say to colleagues at your place of business. If they trail you: Fight for your rights - you will not lose.
Woman	To see her praying: A very good time is coming up. A pregnant woman: You will always have luck with your children. To kiss one: You will gain a lot of money, but be patient. To walk with her: Beware - you can expect a misfortune. To meet a woman with dark hair: Most people envy you. To meet a woman with blond hair: You have a faithful spouse. To argue with one: You are on the brink of an important discovery.
Women's guild	To witness one in a dream: A financial dilemma is on the edge of being resolved.
Wood	To see it burn: Any gambling you do will only result in loss.
Woodcock	To catch one: An offer may give you the opportunity to move to another place. To eat one: Be happy - you are a lucky person.
Wood container	To see one: By pinching pennies you will have enough to live on.
Woodgrouse	To hear one: Someone is spying on you so be cautious.
Woodlouse	To dream about one: Your mental condition right now requires the treatment of a doctor.
Wool	To work with it: Restrictions will soon be lifted. To see white wool: You have too much confidence in people. To see black wool: Secret transactions may help you to overcome an obstacle. To see any garment made of wool: Avoid those who like to chatter.
Worms	To see any: Quarrels with your children are very

possible.
If you have some as fish bait: You are in need, but it will take a long time before somebody lends you a helping hand.

Wrangle
With somebody in your dream: This means don't admit any wrongdoings which you didn't do, just to make peace.

Wreckage
To see one: Your religious faith is strong and finally you will be victorious.

Wren
To see this bird in a dream: You will meet a barefaced liar.

Wrestle
If you dream that you wrestle with somebody: Means that the coming days are not easy.

Wrestler
If you see a wrestling match: If you are looking for a lost person, you will be successful.

Wring out
Some material: You will make some bad deals.

Wrinkles
To have some in your face: You will increase your assets.
To see them on somebody else: Your health is stable and you will live a long life.

Write
To do: Good news from friends.
To see others writing: Don't count too much on your children.
To see beautiful handwriting: You may leave your present location.

Writing case
To open one: You will investigate a mystery.
To carry one: Don't become involved in any adventures. They may cost you a lot of money to recover from them.

Writing-paper
To see some: Your boss has confidence in you. Don't disappoint him.
If you tear off writing paper in a dream: You will lose certain rights.

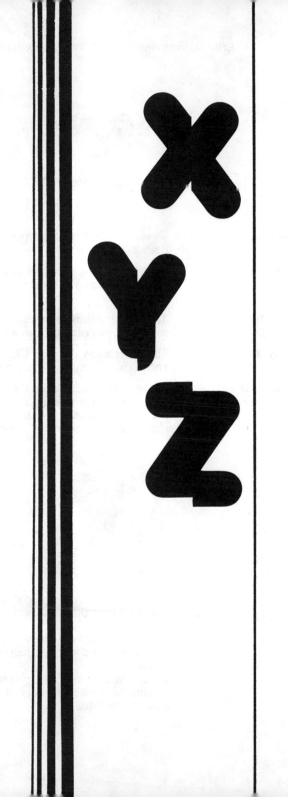

Xantippe

To see one: Nothing is impossible. Don't be despondent.

X-ray

To dream about an x-ray: You may have to accept any terms. You have no chance to do it your way.

X-ray film

To see one: Ailments will respond to the treatment that you obtain from a specialist.

X-ray therapy

To receive x-ray therapy: Carry on as you are and do not change your course.

Xylophone

To hear someone playing the xylophone: If you have a talent for writing, painting, or any other method of expressing your natural talents, you should make good use of these gifts.

Yacht

To sail on one: Do not allow friends who have too much time on their hands to talk you into a vacation.
To see one in a port: The value of your home can be increased with the help of a friend who is a handyman.
To see a yacht race: Start planning now for what you intend to do in the way of work over the next few months.

Yardstick   To dream of a yardstick: You may be in an extravagant mood, but you really cannot afford to splurge at this time.

Yarn   To work with yarn: It would be wise to pay more attention to the personal and private side of your life.
To put it on a spool: You could have a knockout brawl with a loved one that could finish a relationship that has been on and off for some time.

Yeast   To see or buy it: Through ambition and work you will reach a very profitable goal.

Yellow bird   To see one flying: Watch your step when dealing with comparative strangers.
To feed a yellow bird: Make hay while the sun shines.

Yew trees   To see them: The coming days promise to be a pleasant period for home affairs.

Yodel   To hear: Important documents must be signed with care.

Young   To see yourself very young: Don't make a fool out of yourself in front of other people.
To see a teenager: Live your life the way you are now and it will never end.

Yuletide   To dream about yuletide means: Do what you can to be helpful. People will be very grateful to you.

Zebra   To see one: You should spend more time with your family. Also, a slowing down of the pace is indicated.

Zenith   To dream about: You will accomplish the utmost impossibility.

Zeppelin

To see one: Your yearning will be fulfilled.
To ride in one: With courage and education you will reach your goal.
To see one crash: Try to give up everything which is unnecessary. Keep your eyes focused on the future.

Zero

If you see one or numerous: You are in a strong bargaining position. This also means luck in gambling.

Zodiac

To see that sign in a dream: Whatever may happen, the outcome will be in your favor.

Zoological garden

To visit one: It should be possible now to solidify a newly formed relationship with a member of the opposite sex.